PRAISE FOR *LETTERS TO MY GRANDSON*

Why read Bruce Epperly's fifty-two letters to his infant grandson Jack? You might let the preconscious child within yourself wake up to bite-size surprises of grace for complex issues. They're full of humor: Is the little guy really smiling or just passing gas? and pathos: he tells little Jack how his young dad (Bruce's son) deals with cancer and chemo and confides that grandpa didn't get the job he hoped for to live close by. Four generations share bits of joy in Reality.

Kent Ira Groff
Retreat leader, spiritual guide and author of
Honest to God Prayer and Clergy Table Talk
Denver, Colorado

Bruce Epperly's *Letters to My Grandson* is a great read, especially for new grandparents. In a series of fifty-two weekly letters, the author chronicles his growing relationship with his grandson during the first year of the child's life. Epperly's format and conversational style invite new grandparents to join him and form a connection with their own new grandchild on a weekly basis. This book is a great gift for new grandparents.

Besides being a priceless family heirloom for his grandson and subsequent Epperly generations, this book gives new grandparents a recipe for enriching their lives. The recipe begins with a generous helping of love. Knead with plenty of hugs. Combine with prayer and optimism. Mix with music. Add a pinch of perspective. Sprinkle with curiosity. Drizzle with humor. Warm with family fun and play. Then spice it up even more with a dash of special Epperly ingredients.

This gourmet of grandparenting says to new grandparents, See, the baby lies there, a bundle of limitless possibilities and opportunities, waiting to be welcomed by you. Go ahead. Make the first move. Open your arms and heart to new lives: the baby's and yours. You'll never be the same.

Robert C. Grossheider
grandfather, retired English teacher
Cokato, MN

Many of Bruce Epperly's books weave together perceptive theological reflection, practical advice, and sage wisdom. This book of letters to his first grandson creates just such an opportunity to reflect on "big ideas" while offering wholesome advice on the spiritual practice of grandparenting. At 70 years of age, I find myself also fully invested in nurturing my children's children and thinking 'this is one of the great seasons of life.' Bruce is a person who attends carefully to each moment and his writing can crack open an ordinary moment into an expansive probing of the meaning of life – its limitations and pathos or its mysterious wonders and delight.

Riess W. Potterveld
President, Graduate Theological Union
Berkeley, CA

Don't let the title of this book fool you. Bruce Epperly's letters to his grandson provide inspiration for all of us. Between the covers of *Letters to My Grandson*, you will find words that are beautifully and wisely woven together. This book feeds the soul and affirms that the holy may still be found in the simple things of life, like the joy of a grandchild.

As I read *Letters to My Grandson*, I laughed; I cried, and often said out loud, "You got that right, Bruce." He blends the best of many spiritual and religious traditions. It's Epperly at his best ... reflective, humorous, practical, and insightful.

This small but powerful book makes a great morning meditation read. Consider giving it as a gift to a grandparent, a parent, or anyone who values the lessons that deep loving relationships teach us.

Suzanne Adele Schmidt, Ph.D.
Pastor, Trinity UCC, Manchester, MD
Co-Author, *Running on Plenty at Work*

Bruce's weekly letters to his grandson Jack delightfully capture the experience of watching and engaging with your first grandchild in the first year. As a relatively new grandmother, I could feel the joy, love, concern, pain and hope in his reflections. There is a strong sense of constancy and consistency of relationship through the generations that gives us grounding in life. I especially love how Bruce reflects on his own son's early years, Jack's father. Just as strong is the lure to grow, to be curious, to relish life in all its fullness and possibility. It beckons the reader from settled-ness of life to newness and energy of life. The perspective of a grandparent affords space to theologize about God's creative nature and the intentionality needed to nurture a fresh new human being. The insights in this book transcend grandparenting and certainly apply to many relationships, but if you are looking for a gift for a new grandparent, this is it!

Dr. Sharon Rhodes-Wickett
Senior Pastor, Claremont UMC
Claremont, CA

LETTERS TO MY GRANDSON

GAINING WISDOM FROM A FRESH PERSPECTIVE

BRUCE G. EPPERLY

Energion Publications
Gonzalez, FL
2013

ISBN10: 1-938434-75-7
ISBN13: 978-1-938434-75-4
Library of Congress Control Number: 2013949509

Energion Publications
P. O. Box 841
Gonzalez, FL 32560

850-525-3916
energionpubs.com
pubs@energion.com

TABLE OF CONTENTS

A WORD OF THANKS

So glad you're here, so glad you're here
So glad you're here today.
Love brought us here, love brought us here,
Love brought us here, today.

Every page of this book swells with love and gratitude. This is truly a love story describing the relationship of a grandfather and a baby during his first year of life. It celebrates the love of a family, and the wonders of new life brought forth from the bounty of this good earth. Love brings us here and all we can do is say thanks and love each other in response. The circle of love begins with my love for little Jack and extends to my family and those who guided me in the writing of this text.

First of all, I am grateful to my parents, Everett and Loretta Epperly, who taught me the meaning of love, faith, and persistence. I am grateful to my brother, William Everett Epperly, whose soul shined when he heard that Jack's middle name was "Everett" like his own. Bill died in Jack's first year. Jack will never get to know Uncle Bill, but my brother's love will live on in his soul and cells. My heart is filled with joy as I give thanks for my mother-in-law Maxine, just getting started at 95. Thirty five years ago, my wife Kate brought love into my life and together our love brought Jack's father, Matt, into the world, and made it possible for little Jack's shining soul to emerge. She is a wonderful partner in every season of life and now especially in the adventure of grandparenting together. I am grateful to Jack's other grandparents, Bill and Cathy, for their love of Jack and the gift of their daughter Ingrid. My gratitude is boundless to

Matt and Ingrid for inviting us into Jack's life and enabling us to be the grandparents we always dreamed of becoming. Truly, it takes a village to raise a child and support a new family, and we are discovering day by day that we are all in this together.

A handful of friends read this text along the way – Patricia Adams Farmer, Jo Ann Goodson, Nancy Harcourt, and Anna Rollins. I am grateful for their support, comments, and enduring friendship.

Finally, this book is about blessing one little child, but the blessing doesn't end with Jack. As I complete this text, Jack is now two and has a little brother Jamie, who is also a little light in the world. I bless him, too. The blessing of my two grandsons extends to embrace every little child, and that means all of us, especially the children of the world. To be blessed is to know that you are loved, touched, and held in healthy ways, and told that you are unique in the whole universe. Blessing means having enough food, shelter, and health care to nourish body, mind, and spirit. Blessing means living in peace with loved ones, nurtured by parents who do not worry about violence in schools, bombs in the streets, and child slavery and sex trafficking. As I love my little grandson, I am learning that my love for him must grow to embrace all the children of this good earth.

Another children's song says, "Every little soul must shine, must shine, every little soul must shine, must shine." Most of all, I give thanks to you, Jack, for being my inspiration for seeing life from a new perspective. And so, I bless you, little Jack, along with all the little children of the world. May your little soul shine each day of your life, giving light and love to everyone you meet. May you grow loving and strong, and face life's challenges with courage and hope. May you know that life is beautiful and that there is wisdom and love to be found everywhere. Thank you, Jack, for your shining gift of love and life, and for your baby heart that glows with each new morning.

A GREAT ADVENTURE BEGINS

EVERY LITTLE SOUL MUST SHINE

Mr. Rabbit, Mr. Rabbit, your fur is mighty gray,
Yes, dear God, it's made that way.
Every little soul must shine, must shine, must shine.
Every little soul must shine, must shine, must shine.

This book is a love story, but it is also an adventure story. It is the story of the lively and surprising spiritual adventures of a grandfather and his first grandchild. These are adventures that most people overlook, because they occur right under our noses, the most common and most wonderful moments of life.

The philosopher Plato spoke of love as a process of growing wings to soar to the heavens so that we can remember the prenatal beauty we forgot at our birth. This love story is about my grandson Jack's growing his wings of wisdom and beauty, and about the fresh perspectives on life that I learned with Jack as he began to soar during his first year of life. It is also about my being born anew in my late fifties, an aging baby boomer, through learning to experience the world on my knees, creeping and crawling, rolling and bouncing, and dancing and singing with my little grandson. This adventure of spirit is about discovering an enchanted reality in changing diapers, calming a fearful child, and spending a morning looking at fingers and toes and an elephant's nose.

Love grows wings and enables our hearts to soar in so many ways every day. Jewish wisdom says that there is an angel whispering "grow, grow" over every blade of grass. I am sure that an

3

angel is whispering to my grandson Jack, "grow, grow." Creative wisdom, moving well beneath his consciousness and mine, lures him forward moment by moment on this amazing adventure of becoming a child of God on this good Earth.

This year I discovered that same creative wisdom luring me forward. During a year of radical reshaping of my professional life, I experienced hope and possibility as I saw the world from Jack's vantage point and rediscovered the enchantment of each unique moment of experience. I found myself chanting, "grow, grow" as I faced new professional adventures that were matched by my adventures as a grandparent. Jack's gusto in facing novelty inspired me to venture forth toward new personal and professional horizons.

Philosophers, like Plato, have spoken of the moment of birth as a process of losing the memory of one world as we claim the realities of another. While I believe that one life on Earth is enough, this book is about remembering, in this case, my remembering of life on my knees and childhood days of constant discovery. It is about being amazed and enchanted by this wondrous and terrifying world that's all around us – the magic reality of fireflies, melodies and hymns, loving touch, and loud thunder rumbling in the night. It's about gaining wisdom from sharing the fresh perspectives of infants and toddlers for whom the world is new every morning. In fact, their world is new every nanosecond. Wonders greet them, and us, with every sunrise and every breath.

Chinese philosophers speak of every child as an "uncarved block" who is shaped by the experiences he or she has in life. What is exciting for child and grandparent alike is to share deeply in this very moment – this unique and unrepeatable nanosecond of creativity - in which the world is entirely new and full of possibility. Surely, life always is this way, but it's all too often forgotten! What joy it is to remember this novelty bursting forth in the birth of each moment! What joy it is to see the universe through the eyes of a small child! It is truly to discover heaven on earth.

To live daily in what adults call the "real world," we need familiarity and ritual, and we need patterns of behavior and interpretation, and such familiarity is often good. It is certainly necessary if we are to get to work on time, meet friends for dinner, or finish a writing assignment. But, the cost of this familiarity is often a loss of spontaneity, wonder, and creativity. I am reclaiming this sense of spiritual spaciousness as I play alongside Jack, entering his world and discovering something new about my own. As the saying goes, "it's never too late to have a happy childhood." In that spirit, I pray that as you read these words you may experience this same sense of joy at the amazing wonder of life, unfolding and evolving moment by moment, regardless of your age or current life situation.

I am a theologian and pastor by training and disposition. I am interested in the meaning of life, the tension of good and evil, and the difficulty we have in knowing the difference. I am captivated by how things came to be – this whole universe and the little child sleeping in my arms. I enjoy reflecting on whether the universe and the events of our lives contain an inner wisdom and order, at the root, or are just random events, accidental and without purpose. But, an inquisitive theologian without love is, as a spiritual teacher asserted, "noisy gong or a clanging cymbal" (I Corinthians 13:1). Worse than that, a theologian or philosopher without a loving heart risks embracing ideologies that divide and conquer, exclude and judge, and destroy and alienate. The world has enough of such theologians – and politicians - today! In contrast to ideology without love – and I might add prayerful and playful noticing of life as it unfolds - I seek the simple path of childlike wonder and love as I try to see the world from my grandson's perspective. This task is both humbling and inspiring. My heart has grown and softened as I experience the spacious love of his baby heart.

My reflections of my son's first year are neither scientific nor observational, although this book is the fruit of loving observation. Nor is this book a primer on child rearing. It is an adventure story, emerging as I am growing along with my first grandchild. It is a story of creative wisdom, adventure, and beauty. It is the story of the growing love of a grandfather and his grandson. But, I hope it is also an invitation for you to see the simple creativity and wisdom incarnate in every infant's life. It is a reminder to us all that every moment of our lives is new, and complete and beautiful in its own way.

I am also writing this book for Jack and his parents, and parents everywhere. I hope that years from now Jack will pick this book up and remember the wonderful simplicity of this complicated universe. As I am seeing the world from Jack's perspective, I realize how much I've forgotten about my own son's first year. The price we pay for new adventures is letting go of the immediacy of the present moment. Playing with Jack has stimulated my memories of another beautiful little soul, my son Matt, whom I held in my arms some thirty one years ago. These days I am rediscovering that the same creative wisdom that lured my son Matt forward, enlivening his soul as well as his cells, even before he was born, lives on Jack and me.

I send this love story out into the universe and to the One who continues to create in and with us, and finally, as a reminder of the preciousness of life on this good earth and my hope for the future. When I look at Jack, shining brightly with love and possibility, my heart breaks as I remember the thousands of "little Jacks" (both boys and girls) starving in Somalia and throughout the world. I am grief-stricken at the neglect of children in the United States, where one in five children live in poverty and education and health care takes second place to greed and self-interest. I pray for the children in Somalia and all children everywhere who are born into poverty or families in which abuse, neglect, and fear are everyday realities. How blessed it is to be born into a loving family that can feed, clothe, educate, and provide health care for a child!

The love I feel for my grandson extends to embrace our planet and the future he will inherit from my generation and that of his parents. I pray for the healing of this good Earth, and its realities of global climate change, which are, in part, the result of human choices and our failure to see the world from the perspective of the child, filled with wonder, love, and possibility. This love story is a call for every grandparent to work for a world in which joy, laughter, food, love, and security are the rule rather than the exception in every child's life.

Truly this is a glorious day to be alive, and I rejoice in the opportunity to live fully today and everyday as I learn to see the world from a new perspective, through the eyes of a little child, my grandson, Jack Everett Epperly. As you read this text, I pray that you will see the world through the eyes of today's children, for in seeing the world through their eyes you will experience God's dream for your life and this glorious and precious planet. "This is the day that God has made, let us rejoice and be glad in it!" (Psalm 118:24)

WEEK ONE

BIRTH DAY

In the beginning was your birth. It was a hot August day, but that wasn't what was on your mind, Jack. No one quite knows what you experienced in the womb, but I suspect on that day, you knew something amazing was going to happen to you and the world. Many cultures begin counting a child's life at conception and that makes sense to me. For at conception, the moment of the big birth when your parents' sperm and egg unite to bring forth new life, something unique and wonderful happens that cannot be duplicated anywhere else in the universe. A lot of people reduce this wonder of new creation to political bickering and to fruitless questions about "When life begins?" That's not an issue for me to adjudicate, nor does it matter to you today. The really important thing is that sometime nearly ten months ago, an amazing singularity came to being that eventually would burst forth from your mother's womb on a hot August day in 2010.

You're a unique child in so many ways, Jack, first because "you are you." But, second because you are a miracle baby. You are an IVF, in vitro fertilization baby, which means your life came into existence thanks to the work of scientists as well as your parents. Love comes in many ways, sometimes through parents joining with one another in the intimacy of lovemaking; at other times, love emerges through the creativity of physicians and scientists. It doesn't matter how you get here. Just getting here is what counts, and your arrival was a joy, worthy of great celebration. I am certain that God blesses every birth and rejoices in the creation of new life.

When your Grandma Kate and I got the call that your mom and dad had just left for the hospital, we quickly collected our wits and our clothing and, in my case, a few books and my laptop, and zoomed down the highway from Lancaster to Washington D.C. Our hearts were filled with great joy and anticipation. We had been waiting for this moment for nearly a year. I really had no idea what being a grandparent would be like and what my love for you would be like until your mother became pregnant. Your dad, my son Matt, and your mom, Ingrid, became new people when they became pregnant with you. They became people who would nurture and bring forth new life, your little life. Your Grandma Kate and I became new people, too. From now on, we had a new vocation: to love, support, nurture and counsel, you and your parents without any concern for power or control, except the power of love.

When I saw you for the first time, tears filled my eyes. That's when you became "Grandpa's little man" or my "Grandpa-man," for short. You were so very small, yet the whole universe was concentrated into your little life. I believe that God is everywhere and so I saw your little self shining with God's love the first time I saw your face and heard your cries. I believe that every place and every person is a universe in miniature, and that was my feeling as I gazed upon you in your hospital bassinet. There was as much God in that hospital room that day as any "heaven" I can imagine! There was more God in the light that shone from your face than any brick and mortar church, temple, shrine, or mosque can contain. It was the light that gave birth to the universe and shines through every little soul. It was the energy of love made flesh in the busyness of a metropolitan hospital just as it did once upon a time in Bethlehem's stable.

I believe that newborns possess wisdom that comes from another world, a deeper spiritual reality, dynamically moving yet lost to most adults. They have no buffers against the One in whom we live and move and have our being (Acts 17:28). In the womb, they experience truth and holiness; the concreteness of mother's love; they are nourished from the Loving Source of all creativity, and from that life source they learn all the important truths of life. I saw that wisdom in you right away, Jack. It wasn't about facts, but about relationships, the wisdom of knowing you are connected with a life-giving universe.

Newborns remind world-weary adults about one of the first lessons of life: we are connected to a living source of nourishment that will sustain us if we just latch onto it. We don't have to work for it; it's already there. It's the grace of connection – what some spiritual teachers call interdependence - that provides for our deepest needs even when we don't know what we truly need.

To know its abundance, all we need to do is connect! In that first connection, we learn to trust that through the love of our parents and grandparents and then others, the world and the One who brings life into being will supply our deepest needs.

A soul that forgets its connection, or fails to latch on to the sustaining energy of mother's milk, lives a life of fear and isolation. It never has enough. It's always searching for more, sometimes hurting others just to find that sense of connection. It's my job as your grandpa and the job of parents and other loved ones to help you remember that you are always connected and that the most important connection right now is the love that feeds, touches, bathes, changes diapers, and comes when you cry.

But, little man, you already know the truth. Deep down, you know we're connected. Deep down, you know that if we reach out and connect – and help others connect - we can have everything we need and so can everyone else. Maybe that's the most important truth we forget as we move further and further away from womb and breast and parents' care. Over the years, we need to establish our identity, to rejoice in our uniqueness, and that requires distance and space from those who have nurtured us. But discovering our uniqueness is always the gift of loving connection and the trust that gives us confidence to love, create, and grow.

Rejoice with me, Jack, that you are here, and that we are connected. You are alive and it is good! Cry with vigor and sleep in peace. Love brought you here, and love will surround you every day. Love just wants you to reach out and connect.

Love, Grandpa Bruce

WEEK TWO

LATCHING ON

I want to continue last week's conversation on relationships and connection. Jack, each day you are teaching me that we are all connected with each other. The truth is that from the very beginning of life, we depend on other people to provide us with safe and nurturing environments. First, you need your mom. Your mother is your whole universe from the time of your conception and extending to the first few weeks of your life. In the womb, you get everything you need to grow and prepare for your birth into outer world. Long before you were born, she loved you. For months, she practiced for your birth – eating right, exercising, resting, and loving the growing life within her. She even passed up on her favorite beverage – strong caffein-ated lattes – so that you would be healthy.

Your dad hasn't been absent. He's been loving your mom by rubbing her back, buying groceries, and singing silly songs to you in your mother's womb. Your dad has even gained a few pounds to be in synch with your mother! No doubt you heard echoes of his words, vibrating in the womb, "I love the monkey-chew. I love the monkey chew. The monkey chew is you." And, oh how your mom and dad loved you when you burst forth, red-faced and crying, "I'm here and ready for love."

After you're born, you still need your mom. You're still con-nected but once you're born you need to claim it. That's what latching on is about. It's about finding your mother's breasts, or for some, a parent's bottle, so you can receive their love, flowing through the milk or formula that nurtures your growth.

The world begins with your mother's love. In latching on, you learn that life is good and people can be trusted. The psychologist Erik Erikson described our first moments of latching on and being held as the source of basic trust, our belief that the world can be trusted to support our basic needs for survival, protection, and nurture. As you get older, your circle of latching on will become wider and wider. You'll find other people to latch onto – people you can trust to respond to your needs. As the circle continues to grow, it will include your dad, then Grandma and me, Grandpa Bill and Grandma Cathy, and other caregivers. Later your circle will grow even wider to include friends you can depend on, and they'll depend on you, and then a partner with whom you'll want to spend your life. You'll latch on to her or him, and he or she will latch onto you to receive the joys of life. But, to get that nurture you must reach out. You must connect. Trust must be embraced and accepted from that first moment when you discovered that you had the power to create connections of your own.

Someday, you may have a baby of your own, a little boy or girl, who will need your love for nurture and protection. You'll be the world to that child and they'll learn to latch onto you and your partner with whom you will love this new little soul into life.

Life is all about latching on, whether to a breast or a bottle. We all need each other to thrive and grow. Life is about giving and receiving in relationships. A happy life is about reaching out to receive the nurture you need and learning to be as trustworthy as your mom and dad were when you depended on them completely. The love that helps you latch on as a baby will teach you how to give love when you're older and people depend on you.

It's a great responsibility to love and care for others, and right now you're getting nurture that will last a lifetime. You don't need to do anything right now, except reach out to receive the love your mom and dad and the rest of us have for you. So latch on to life, little man. When you latch on to your mom, you are teaching me now as an adult in late midlife to reach out for what I need and to accept the nurture all around me. You are blessed, little grandson, and I am blessed to be with you.

Love, Grandpa Bruce

WEEK THREE

SLEEPING IN GRANDPA'S ARMS

Until you came along, Jack, I had forgotten how great it felt to have a baby sleep in my arms. It's been over thirty years since your dad was a baby in my arms. Like you, Jack, your dad was a healthy good natured baby. He nestled in my arms for hours as we sat together beside the pot-bellied wood stove in our home in Mount Pleasant, Michigan. In our little flat, your dad learned to crawl and walk and eat solid food. He laughed a lot just like you will when you are a little older.

Well, Jack, it will be awhile before you crawl and walk, but that day will come soon enough. You will grow steadily and quietly, guided by wise and creative forces within you, learning and doing new things, and exploring new possibilities. You will discover that life is full of possibilities that pull you forward to the next step in your journey. Most of the time, what is pulling you forward is invisible and imperceptible but you will grow just the same. With the right caring and support, you will discover that the universe is graceful. There is an inner wisdom and harmony that will give you what you need and just when you need it and you don't have to do anything to receive its gifts of health, energy, and balance.

But today, all you have to do is sleep. You've been in my arms for two hours, and for the past two hours I've done nothing except look lovingly at you, and remember when your dad was a wee one, too. Holding you is like meditating. I focus only on one thing at a time and discover that time slows down and my previous commitments fall into the background, at least for

15

those two precious hours. I have discovered that although going to work, writing books, and financially supporting my family are important, love – mediated by a gentle and affirming embrace – is what's most important in life.

Sleep is good. I don't sleep much. I meditate instead. I stay up relatively late and then get up at 5:00 a.m. to pray, walk, and write. But there's something good about simply resting, feeling your body relax, and letting go of the need to do anything but rest into the present moment in a way that refreshes our souls like nothing else. I like the process of falling to sleep, of feeling yourself grow tired and then, without noticing how you got there, you discover you've wakened to a new day.

Meditating can help you relax into the present moment, too. Later on, I'll teach you how to meditate, but for now just enjoy sleeping in your grandpa's arms. You don't have to do anything but rest in my arms, knowing that I will watch over you. I will nurture you. I will protect you from harm. And, I will help you grow. Those are my promises to you. I will be for you God's grace with loving arms.

Even though I raised your dad, it's a great honor for your parents let me hold you these days. I know that when they're weary from getting up at night, it gives them a break. But, more than that, they trust me with their life's most precious gift, and that means the world to me. So tonight as you rest, know that your mom and dad and grandma and I will always love you and give you our best – a touch, a kiss, a safe place, and the love of a lifetime. You have my word on that. Just as I've loved your dad through health and sickness and in joy and sorrow, I will love you forever and I will do all I can to make your world a safe and beautiful place, so that you can live with joy and trust and love all the days of your life.

Love, Grandpa Bruce

WEEK FOUR

WATCH THE BABY'S NECK

For the first few weeks, your dad – my son – has been telling me, "Watch the baby's neck" whenever I pick you up. I find this very funny. Sometimes I say to him, "Guess what, Son, I've done this before. I picked you up as an infant and somehow you made it safely through your childhood and now you are here to tell me what to do! Give me a break!"

But, Jack, please know I appreciate your dad's protectiveness. He is the number one man in your life and the number one man in my life, and I'm here to support him in caring for you in any way I can. He wants you to be safe and healthy, and so do I. Even though you're a hearty young fellow, you still need to be handled with care. We are all stronger than we think, but we're also much more easily hurt, both physically and emotionally, than we realize.

These days I'm reading a book entitled *Baby Hearts*. Reading this reminds me that right now, Jack, you're all heart. You don't have words for it yet, but you pick up the emotions of those around you. That means we have to be careful to insure that the emotions you pick up are healthy and loving. We have to watch not only your neck, but also your heart!

Trust is the key to a happy life, and we learn about trust primarily by being supported in the first year or so of life. Trust includes the feeling that the world is a good place and the important people in your life consistently care for you and won't "jerk you around" too much. With the right support, you will learn that you can do good things and make a difference in the world. Consistent support of your neck and your heart gives you a sense that even when things don't go well and unexpected things happen, you will have the ability to bounce back and respond creatively.

So, watching out to support your little neck is a big deal! It's not just about your physical wellbeing but about knowing that you are safe and cared for. It's about creating an environment of stability and consistency that will surround you in a world in which everything within you and outside of you is changing.

Life will jerk you around. It jerks everyone around sooner or later. People aren't always considerate and sometimes they will hurt you by words or actions. When we take care of you now, we are building a foundation that will help you take care of yourself in an uncertain world. When you're older, you may have to "watch your own neck" and find a place of strength and safety within yourself when the world seems undependable. Hopefully, our consistency of love and care will help you find that strength within when you most need it. It all begins with watching your neck!

Love, Grandpa Bruce

WEEK FIVE

OPENING YOUR EYES
TO THE WORLD

In your first few weeks of life, eating and sleeping and being held and kept warm were enough for you. But, as the days unfold, you're beginning to make contact with a wider world. You're opening your eyes for more than just a few seconds. You're keeping them open for minutes a time, trying to make sense of the outer world that sustains and surprises you.

The world is a confusing place, at first, with all of the many colors, shapes, and sounds flowing all around you. At this point, you don't really know the difference between yourself and others. We don't mind that because we know that our job right now is to be your connection with the world, your source of nurture and protection. But, as your eyes mature and focus, you'll see more of the world. You'll begin to understand that there is a big and surprising world outside your mom and dad and grandparents.

Everyday I can tell that you're noticing more, Jack. And these days, I'm trying to notice more, too. I'm trying to see the world through your eyes – the eyes of freshness and wonder. Sometimes, I think grownups quit noticing the world in all its wonder, variety, and change. They see the same old things, thinking that nothing changes, and miss the novelty and beauty of each new day. We think we've got it figured out, but nothing is further from the truth. All around us, life is changing and each moment brings new adventures into unknown territory. You can walk by the same spot each day and then one day you see it for what it is – beautiful, infinite, and amazing! You see, as if for the first time, the setting sun shining through a tree, the darting of a firefly on a summer's evening, or a bee on a flower, and everything has changed for you. Or, you look at your child or partner, and suddenly see them with new eyes. You discover a smile or a tear that you'd overlooked.

Embracing the newness of each moment is the lesson I'm learning from you. As I look at you, I'm learning to pause and notice, and then open my heart to the world around me.

Thank you, Jack, for helping me see the world with new eyes. The newness of your life every morning helps mine to be new, too. You constantly see and do new things, and when I'm with you, I do too. Today is a new day, and with you in my life I look forward to the adventures of today and tomorrow with great expectation. I'm on the lookout now for the smallest of things, recognizing that the whole universe is packed into every infant and firefly.

The Zen Buddhists call this meeting the world with the beginner's mind. Jesus called it considering the lilies and how they grow. I call it seeing the world with the beginner's eye: experiencing the world moment by moment in all its radiance, wonder, and novelty, and rejoicing and giving thanks for each new day. This "beginner's eye" helps me celebrate life as I have never done before!

I'm learning to "see" anew as I simply carry you around the living room, or take you into the garden, or walk down the street with you in my arms. When I open my eyes in the morning, I think of you – and rejoice at the amazing newness of every day. You are alive, and I'm glad to be alive! What a miracle it is that we are both here in this time and place! As a holy person once said, "This is the day that God has made, and I will rejoice and be glad in it." (Psalm 118:24) I rejoice to be your companion on the marvelous and constantly changing journey of each new day.

Love, Grandpa Bruce

WEEK SIX

IS IT A SMILE OR IS IT GAS?

It's clear to me that you're smiling a lot these days. At least, that's what I think whenever I see those lips of yours curling into that "I'm happy with the world" look. I realize that a debate rages on between those who rejoice in their smiling babies and those who claim that the upturned corners of your mouth are just a sign that you are releasing gas.

Well, when in doubt, I go online to find the answers. This morning I spent an hour online, researching why infants smile, and I discovered that most baby smiles are not caused by gas. Dr. Daniel Messinger says that "babies smile when they're asleep from birth [onward]." Sadly, in my opinion, he also adds that for first month or two, a baby's smiles have no emotional content.[1] Well, he may be right about babies smiling when they're asleep. I know adults do, so why not babies? But, I'm not so sure that a baby's smiles are totally automatic with no emotional content. How can we know? To assume that there's no emotional content in a baby's smile somehow artificially separates your emotions from your body. It assumes that there is no relationship between the way we feel and our facial gestures, even as infants. I believe that everything fits together – mind, body, and

---

1 http://www.justthefactsbaby.com/baby/article/why-babies-smile/92

spirit and that, as scientist Candace Pert says, the "molecules of emotion" are everywhere in your body.[2]

The first week of your life when you were in NICU (neonatal intensive care) on oxygen and antibiotics to clear some fluid from your lungs, your eyes certainly looked sad. But, when you got home, you glowed with happiness. Now, I know that our mood had changed from worried to happy, but I suspect yours did too, when you began to feel better and were in the quiet comfort of your parents' home rather than the high tech world of intensive care.

I believe everything in our lives fits together, not only our emotions and body, but our relationship with the wider world of plants, animals, and oceans. I believe that when you're happy, you show it, Jack, even if you don't have words to describe how you feel. It is an energy that the Celts in Scotland and Ireland describe as the "glow flow." Your happiness flows through every cell in your body. As the song goes, "if you're happy and you know it, then your face will surely show it! If you're happy and you know it, clap your hands!"

So I say that when you smile, you're really happy, Jack, and I'm glad you smile a lot. I think it's the happiness of being warm and dry and well fed and held in loving arms. I suspect it's like being back in your mother's tummy – feeling comfortable, safe, and secure. But, I also think that as you get to know the world better and you begin to interact with it more, you will respond to your mom and dad's voices and touch, with a smile that mirrors what's inside you, showing all the world – "I'm feeling good and I'm glad you're here with me" even when you have no thoughts or words to express it. You're happy because the people around you are happy!

Now, Jack, I guess by now you know that I'm a teacher and a writer. I love words and ideas. I spend most of my day imagining

2 Candace Pert, *The Molecules of Emotion: The Science Behind Mind-Body Medicine* (New York: Simon and Schuster, 1999).

new possibilities for writing and teaching and helping people be healthy and happy in the work they do. But you have taught me that words and thoughts are often overrated in our society. They're often only a small part of what we experience. I believe that there's a wealth of emotion that flows through every cell of your body. Your whole body, not just your face and eyes, show us how you feel.

Sharing your feelings is one of the most important things in life. At first, maybe just expressing how you feel with a squeal of delight or a cry of discomfort is just good enough. Later on, you will have words to describe how you feel, but don't let them get in the way. Remember that feeling good is good even if you can't explain why.

And remember to share your feelings – good and bad. We want to hear them and respond to them.

Jack, regardless of what the experts say, I choose to believe that you're smiling because right now at six weeks old you experience the world as a good place. You "know" deep down that you're loved. You're fed and held and that's about as good as it gets now. A very wise man, the Dalai Lama, once said that one of the greatest things in life is to be born into loving arms and to die into loving arms. Another wise man, Paul of Tarsus, said nothing can separate us from God's love. (Romans 8:38-39) We'll not talk about the death part for awhile. But, one thing I'm certain about is that you were born into loving arms that first day, when your mom and dad and grandma and I first held you. Loving arms have embraced you all your life and I think that's why you smile. Your smiling makes me smile and I thank you for sharing the joy you feel as the goodness of life.

Love, Grandpa Bruce

WEEK SEVEN

BATH TIME AND BEDTIME

To me, a happy life involves the right blend of order and chaos, familiar and unfamiliar, and surprise and regularity. If every day was predictable, life would be boring. We'd never grow and learn new things. But, if nothing was the same, we would have to start all over moment by moment. You wouldn't be able to crawl down the hallway or eat your breakfast or recognize your mom and dad as special people. Things we repeat over and over again are called "rituals." A good life involves rituals that provide order and stability amid the joyful and sometimes chaotic changes of life.

Your mom and dad have established a bedtime ritual that's working for you right now. Just before your nighttime nursing, they give you a bath. You really enjoy your bath time, Jack. Small as you are, you kick and splash around and make squealing sounds. Then, after a little massage with lavender lotion and a cozy swaddle is put around you, it's time for your mom to take you to the rocking chair where you fall asleep nursing in her arms, happy, content, and well fed. Bath, bed, breast, and beyond!

I like baths and showers, too, Jack. But, mine are usually at the beginning of the day after my morning walk. I enjoy the ritual of washing myself and feeling the water splashing on my skin. I delight in that good clean feeling you get after a shower or bath. After a good shower, I feel alive and renewed and ready for whatever comes next. Life is adventurous for both you and me, and rituals of baths and showers give us a chance for a fresh start – either to bed or to work.

You know, when I'm feeling sick, I love to take a bath. I lay back and let the water cover me. The warm water comforts me. I begin to feel better almost immediately. Maybe it's because it reminds me of a time when I was a little child and my parents took care of me or, maybe, it brings back some ancient memory, an earlier time when I enjoyed the peaceful warmth of my mother's womb. I am an adult now and can take care of myself, at least most of the time, but like most people, there's always a small child inside who needs reassurance and care when life is difficult and we're not feeling well.

Daily rituals calm and soothe. I have a lot of them. Physician Herbert Benson speaks of rituals as bringing out the "relaxation response." When we repeat certain behaviors like focusing on a special word or our breathing, our bodies grow calm and relaxed. Our blood pressure goes down and we enter a state of peaceful alertness, almost like being asleep, but we're wide awake. I think you experience that same relaxation response whenever you take a bath, get a massage, latch on to your mom's breast, or snuggle up in our arms.

Rituals make up a big part of my life. Every morning before sunrise, I begin my day with twenty minutes of quiet meditation, before taking a long walk through our neighborhood. While I'm walking, I say a prayer for you and the people I love. In my prayers, I send happy and healthy energy your way and surround you and your parents with love. After I finish my morning rituals, I feel calm, relaxed, creative, and energized. When I get home, I'm ready to meet the challenges of a new day with courage and calm in my heart.

I have other rituals that I live by. Every afternoon, I have a strong cup of coffee, just like I do in the morning when I begin to write. Every night, I give your grandma a back rub and tell her I love her. Before I go to sleep, I review the day. I think of the good things that have happened and the people I love. Then, I tell myself a bedtime story. I visualize talks I'll be giving and places I intend to go. Before I know it, I'm fast asleep. In a few months, I'll be telling you stories when you go to bed – tales of dinosaurs and lions and things we did today. Someday, when you're a little older, I'll read stories to you about space ships and mysteries like I did with your dad. We'll learn about Winnie the Pool and Piglet and Thomas the Train! We may just talk awhile about what's on your mind and what you did today. Those will be our nighttime rituals.

Yes, rituals are good. They are road signs that help us navigate the changes of life with confidence and joy. So, enjoy your bath, your nightly massages, our embraces, and your mom's breast. May your days and nights be filled with rituals of love as well as lots of surprises.

Love, Grandpa Bruce

WEEK EIGHT

LOOKING AT YOUR HANDS

You've discovered your hands, Jack. This morning you spent nearly an hour examining your hands, moving them from to side to side, and turning them over and over. You were investigating your fingers as you opened and closed them time after time. You are noticing that you have big strong hands with long fingers like your mom's. Somehow you're beginning to notice your body. And, you're noticing that you can do all sorts of things with your body. It's your body, and not someone else's. In the whole universe, no one has hands like you. Nobody has your body, your fingerprints, or your skin. You are unique and so is every other child.

Hands are marvelous things, Jack. In a few months, you'll discover that you can hold a bottle to feed yourself, throw a ball, and hold your parents' hands when you walk on the sidewalk.

Hands are meant for feeling the world. They are meant for noticing textures and keeping you safe. Some things are soft, other things are hard. Some things are prickly and sharp and if you touch them, you'll feel pain. Other things are smooth and soft to the touch like down comforters or your mom's face.

Your hands are meant for touching people you love. You are flourishing because your mom and dad and other caring people like me touch you all day long. We greeted you with loving hands the moment you were born. We hold you and caress you, skin on skin, letting you know by our touch that you are loved. We rock you to sleep and pick you up when you're crying. Touch is wonderful and babies can't live without it. Caring touch nourishes you just as much as breast milk, your mother's smile, and sunshine in the morning.

One of my greatest joys is holding you, Jack. I love to hold you against my chest so that you can hear my heartbeat, and I can hear your gentle breathing. Sometimes you fall asleep in my arms, pressed against my chest, and life feels especially good for both of us. Our breaths become in synch with each other and the breathing of the universe. I like to pat you on the back when I walk you around the house, rocking you back and forth. I like to put my hand on the top of your smooth, blond head, to feel your energy, bless you, and pray that your life will be healthy and beautiful.

Sometimes, when I'm holding you in my arms, I'm reminded of another little boy, your dad, who fell asleep in my arms just like you. It was thirty years ago, but it feels like yesterday.

When you're older, you'll learn what it's like to enjoy touching other people. You'll learn the difference between rough and gentle touch. "Cara, cara" your mom says to remind you to be gentle with your touch. You'll learn to share your love by patting people on the back, putting your arms around their necks, caressing their bodies, and holding their hands. And, it will feel good for both of you.

Touching reminds us how good it is for us to have a body, not just any body – but your body. Your body is beautiful just the way it is. And, so is everyone else's body. Bodies are made to be loved and touched with respect.

As you grow older, you'll discover that some people use their hands to hurt other people. They push and punch and prod and poke. Sometimes you may have to push back when someone attacks you or hurts someone you love. You may have to tell your parents or a teacher when someone touches you in a way that makes you feel uncomfortable. Hands can be used for hate and violence, but hands and arms are intended for loving and helping, and keeping you safe.

Jack, I know that you will grow to be an affectionate young man. You've been surrounded by love all your life and this love will always light your way. And, in the years ahead, you will learn to give love by touching and being touched, and helping others feel safe and loved just like you're feeling right now as I hold you in my arms.

Love, Grandpa Bruce

WEEK NINE

TURNING AWAY

I've been reading a lot about child development lately. I want to understand what's going on in your evergrowing body, mind, and spirit. One text suggests that when infants turn away from people or bury their heads in their caregiver's chest, they are trying to get a little peace and quiet in an amazingly complex and chaotic world. You turn away from new people Jack, but usually not for long. When you're a few months old, every face – other than your mom and dad's - is "new." Sometimes when a number of people come to visit, it's just too noisy. There's simply too much stimulation from too many faces. So you turn away. We all love you, but sometimes it's just too much for you to take at one time!

Sometimes you even turn away when I speak to you, but I don't take it personally. I know that you just need a little space and time to make sense of your world.

Even at two months, you're discovering that a healthy life requires the right blend of sound and silence, action and contemplation, and movement and rest. You can't be active all the time, nor can you spend all your time in being with other people. Turning away from too much stimulation is built into who you are. We all need a little space to "regroup" to prepare for our next adventures!

Later on, Jack, I hope you will learn to do a type of withdrawal called "meditation." Silence is one of the ways that I get space to listen to my own needs, and imagine possibilities for the future. Meditating gives me a sense of peace that connects me with the creative impulses of the world around me in nature and other people. When you're a little older, I may teach you some of the meditation practices that are important to me. But, the practice of meditation begins by just being still and listening – to yourself and the life flowing through you. You are already practicing a type of meditation by "going within" when you turn away.

You may even learn to have a special place in the house where you go just to be by yourself. When I was a little boy, I put a blanket over a card table in my room. I hid under the table and played with my toys. I had a little sanctuary away from my brother and my parents when I needed some space to be with myself.

Now, according to one survey, the Myers Briggs Type Indicator, I'm what is described an introvert. I get my energy from quiet time, writing, and being alone, even though I make my living teaching and speaking in front of groups of people. In contrast, people who are called extroverts get their energy from being around people. Too much alone time can be boring for people who love conversation, action, and relationships. Your Grandma Kate is an extrovert; she loves groups and being around people. She gets her best ideas when she's talking with someone. But, she needs quiet time, too, as a way of connecting with her personal center. I love relationships and conversation, but I need moments of quiet to recharge and restore my spirit.

So from the very beginning of life, we each need to find the right blend of action and reflection and quiet alone time and noisy social times that fit our personality. We all need social, intellectual, and physical stimulation.   But, we also need stillness and time alone in which we relax and let go of our thoughts and worries. Some scientists say that when babies like you, Jack, are asleep, their minds are whirring with action, processing all the things they have learned during the day. Even when you're older, you'll still need quiet time to relax, sleep, and let things sink in.

So feel free to turn away from me and other people when life becomes just too much for you. Take time for yourself. Whether you're an introvert or extrovert, give yourself a little space to be alone and rest. Later, I know you will joyfully plunge forward to embrace the excitement of every new moment with courage and energy.

Love, Grandpa Bruce

WEEK TEN

CENTERING PRAYER, OR HOW TO PUT A BABY TO BED!

Your mom, dad, grandma, and Grandpa Bill have found an interesting way to help you go to sleep when you're having trouble closing your eyes at bedtime. They chant a sacred word, "Aum." Aum or Om is a word in Sanskrit, an ancient language used in the Hindu religion, to describe the energy of life and creation. When you say the word Aum, you join your spirit with the Spirit of the Universe, the Life and Light that flows through all things from stars above to the light of love in the eyes of little babies and their adoring parents.

Wise people say that chanting "Aum" or "Love" or "Jesus" creates an environment of peace. That seems to work for you at bedtime, Jack. Even on your most difficult nights, taking slow deep breaths and saying "Aum" calms you down and helps you rest in your parents' arms, ready for a good night's sleep. Saying "Aum" also calms your parents down, because you know parents can get anxious when their babies can't sleep, and that doesn't help the baby at all! While my centering prayer is different – it involves opening to the light of God – all authentic spirituality opens us to God's calming presence, even when we're tired or crying.

The sounds and meanings of words are important. When you get older, you will discover that people use all sorts of different words to describe the Spirit of Life. They use words like

"God," "Jesus," "Spirit," and "Allah" to describe what's most important to them and what gives them courage, energy, and love. Each word points to something different but they all share a sense of reverence for the universe and the gifts of life and love we receive.

Your parents and grandparents were all raised Christian. For Grandma Kate and me, being part of a religion is an exciting invitation to adventure. For us, being Christian means learning from other peoples' religions as well as about our own faith tradition. It means being awake to the beauty of life and love in all creation and all people, and seeing God in all things and all things in God. It also inspires us to learn from scientists, artists, and historians and people from all walks of life and na-tions. We live in an amazing universe, billions of years old with more galaxies and planets than anyone can count or imagine. So, there's plenty of room for learning new things about life, love, and spirituality.

Aum is not a Christian word, but it expresses our belief in the creative energy that gives life to everything from galaxies, planets, and precious little babies like you. Saying "Aum" is a form of prayer, and I pray a lot, Jack. I use words like "God" and "Jesus" in my prayers. I pray for you, for my close friends, for your mom and dad, for Kate and Grammy (Great Grandma Max) every day. I pray for the world and all the little children. I pray for our president, Barack Obama, and I pray for the leaders of the world's nations. Prayer calms and connects. It reminds me that everything is related and that we need one another to grow, learn, and love. I pray for justice and peace and wholeness for all. People of different faiths may use different words, but it all comes down to finding a sense of holy connection with all of life.

Maybe when you're older, you'll chant your prayers or pray to "Jesus," or "God." These are all good words and they can feed your spirit. There are many other sacred words that will help you connect with the love and light that is all around you and in you. These words will give you a sense of peace, hope, and strength as you do new things and face the challenges of growing up. So, regardless of the words we use, Jack, I and your grandparents pray for you always that the peaceful energy of the universe surround and nurture you and all the children of the world. And each day, I remember you in prayers from my own tradition: the prayer of Aaron and Moses, Mary the mother of Jesus, and Jesus: "May Lord bless you and keep you; the Lord make his face to shine upon you, and be gracious to you; the Lord lift up his countenance upon you, and give you peace." (Numbers 6:24-26) Amen.

Love, Grandpa Bruce

WEEK ELEVEN

MUSIC ALL DAY LONG

Jack, you're a boy who loves music. You love dancing around with your dad to the songs of Country Western singer Keith Urban and listening to folk singer Elizabeth Mitchell.[3] Music seems to calm you when you're cranky and makes you smile when you are sad. At bedtime, I hum to you a tune I sung with your dad when he was young. Grandma Kate sings *You are My Sunshine* and *Somewhere over the Rainbow* as she rocks you in her arms.

One of our favorites is a song by Elizabeth Mitchell. We've been listening to it every morning these days. It's based on a hymn by the Gospel singer Bess Jones. It expresses how I feel whenever I walk in the door to see you after driving two a half hours from Lancaster.

So glad I'm here
So glad I'm here
So glad I'm here today.
So glad I'm here
So glad I'm here
So glad I'm here every day....
Love brought me here
Love brought me here
Love brought me here today.
Love brought me here

---

3 For more on Elizabeth Mitchell, see www.youaremyflower.org

37

Love brought me here
Love brought me here every day....
I'll sing while I'm here
I'll sing while I'm here
I'll sing while I'm here today.
I'll sing while I'm here
I'll sing while I'm here
I'll sing while I'm here every day....
Joy brought me here
Joy brought me here
Joy brought me here today.
Joy brought me here
Joy brought me here
Joy brought me here every day.

Yes, love brings me here every day! It's the love of God and the love in my heart for you. It's fun when Grandma and I sing songs that we sang to your dad when he was a little boy. Our favorites when your dad was small were: *You are My Sunshine*, *Teddy Bear's Picnic*, *Frog Went a Courting*, *Inchworm*, and *This Little Light of Mine*. Of course, we sang and make the hand motions for *Itsy Bitsy Spider*, too! And we sing all of these with you these days.

When you're older, Jack, you'll discover that you can chart your life by the songs you sing and listen to. They'll come from all over the world and be in all sorts of languages. Some will be sad, others will be joyful. Through it all, I hope you learn to have a song in your heart every day, because as the song says, "love brought you here every day!"

Love, Grandpa Bruce

WEEK TWELVE

MORNING PRAYERS

There are literally thousands of ways to pray. Some people use words. Other people use images. Some people sing their prayers or reach out their hands to share healing energy. Still others spend time in silence, just listening for inner guidance. At one time or another, I use all of these, especially when I pray for you, Jack, as I do every morning and throughout the day.

What is prayer? Prayer is about paying attention to your life. It's about pausing and noticing what's all around you and what's inside you. You don't need words to pray. You just need to be aware of what's going on right now in your heart and in the world. Sometimes you just need to breathe and give thanks for each breath you take.

I believe that babies pray whenever they cry out for help or attention. You know when you need something, Jack, and that you must depend on others to respond to your needs. When you cry out, that surely is a prayer to the universe to get what you need!

Every morning, Jack, you and I take time for our own kind of morning prayers. When I hear you wake up early in the morning before anyone else is awake, the first thing I do is pick you up and give you a big hug, and talk with you as I change your diaper. We notice "Mr. Lion" and "Mr. Monkey" and "Mr. Elephant" on the wall of your nursery above your changing table. They are always there. They are your "friends." You think Mr. Elephant's pretty funny and laugh every time I mention his name. Then we go downstairs and open the front door so you can touch the glass, and notice whether it's hot or cold outside. When there aren't too many mosquitoes, we sit on the front porch and look out at the neighborhood. We contemplate the songs of the birds as they wake up and listen to the sounds of the city as people begin their day.

After a few minutes, I walk down the street with you in my arms, and all we do is just notice things. At three months, your eyes are starting to focus and you're seeing new things every day. Sometimes we stop, look, and listen. I share my thoughts with you, Jack. I tell you about the trees and bushes and birds. Together, we discover what a beautiful world we live in. The smallest things in life – little babies and bright flowers – can show us what life's really like. A poet named William Blake said that you can see the universe in a grain of sand. He also said that when we truly experience life in its fullness, we discover that everything is infinite and deserves our reverence and respect. When we take time for our morning prayers, I know that Blake is right.

As I said earlier, things we repeat on a regular basis are called rituals. Things we do over and over shape our lives. Right before bedtime, you take a bath. It prepares you for a good night's sleep. Taking time to pause and notice the world when the day begins is a ritual that's important to me. One of my best friends, Patricia Adams Farmer, is a writer who counsels that we can begin the day with a beauty break and that taking time for beauty shapes the rest of the day. When we start the day with beauty and gratitude, everything seems to go better. When I'm home and as I leave the house for my early morning walk, I sing out the words of a spiritual poem from the Bible, "This is the day that God has made and I will rejoice and be glad in it!" This helps me begin each day with a good attitude and respond to what happens with humor and care rather than irritation and anger. I wonder what happy affirmation you will learn to have in the morning, Jack.

As you grow up, your mornings will get busy. You'll go to day care and later to school. You won't have time for leisurely mornings with me, except during holidays. But I hope that you will remember our early morning "beauty breaks" and take some time each day to pause and notice the wonder of life. I hope you will take time to notice the goodness of each day. May you give thanks for the people who love you and the chance to do something interesting, exciting, and fun every day. That's my prayer for you!

Love, Grandpa Bruce

WEEK THIRTEEN

HOPALONG YOGI

For the past few weeks, your mom has been taking you to "Itsy Bitsy Yoga" classes. Look at you, Jack, you're only three months old and you're already a yogi! I think this is a wonderful idea. Your mom and dad practice yoga at home to promote their well-being and reduce stress. It helps them stay calm with all the changes that you are bringing into their lives. Yoga is all about experiencing energy and peace and love. I believe that anyone can do yoga or Tai Chi, regardless of what faith they affirm.

It's never too early to begin a pathway to health and wholeness that embraces every part of your life, mind, body, spirit, and relationships. Just having your mom help you with gentle stretches or roll you back and forth is good for your health now and later. I hope that when you're a little older and able to understand how to do yoga that your parents will teach you some basic positions. Health of body, mind, and spirit is a habit – something you do every day - and it involves making the thoughtful decisions about what you eat, your attitude towards time, getting enough exercise, and learning how to face life's challenges without getting stressed out. Health is about feeling a sense of peace regardless of what's going on around you, and sometimes, inside you.

Your mom has been singing a song to you that you both learned in class. As she bounces you on her knee rapidly, she sings:

Hopalong yogi, hopalong.

Hopalong, yogi, hopalong .
Go real fast.

When she bounces you slowly, she sings:

Hopalong yogi, hopalong.
Hopalong, yogi, hopalong.
Go real slow.

When you're older, I will teach you to meditate the way I do. I talked to you about this earlier, but this is so important that it deserves repeating. Remember, meditation is about slowing down and focusing on the quiet, gentle spirit within you and the world. When I meditate, I close my eyes, sit still and take a few slow deep breaths. These days I have been focusing on the phrase, "God's light," as I inhale and exhale. Sometimes when I'm walking or sitting with my eyes open, I breathe deeply and say to myself "I breathe the Spirit deeply in and give it out again." For me, Spirit is what gives us energy, wisdom, and love. Spirit is in all of us as the power that gives life, energy, and health in all things. Spirit connects us to one another even though each of us is unique.

In many ways meditation comes naturally for babies. In a few months, you will focus on some object – a leaf, a ball, a piece of paper, or a flower – turning it over and over trying to discover what it is. Meditation is about pausing to notice what's going on in your life and the life around you. Yoga and meditation help you to be fully open to the present moment. They help you experience healthy energy flowing through you from your head to your toes.

Grandma Kate and I look forward to sharing the wisdom we've learned over the years so that you can live creatively and lovingly in a world that will be constantly changing. I pray that you will always be able to find a peaceful, still point around which to shape your life.

Love, Grandpa Bruce

WEEK FOURTEEN

THANKSGIVING

Everyone has come to our house for Thanksgiving this year. Our home in Lancaster is midway between New York, where your mom's parents live and your parents' home in Washington DC. Your mom and dad, Grandma Cathy and Grandpa Bill, Aunt Karen, Uncle Mauro, and your cousins Chiaro and Lucio, Uncle Bill, Grammy Max, and your Grandma Kate and I are all here. We have a big fire in our wood stove and lots of food to eat. Our house is warm from the fire and from all the love that's gathered there. We have each other, and that's the best thing!

Every country has its days of thanksgiving and in our country, the United States of America, Thanksgiving is always toward the end of November. It is a time to remember all the gifts of life we have as Americans — living in a free country and having a safe home, loving parents, good food, opportunities to learn and grow, and so much more.

A wise man, Meister Eckhardt, once said that "if the only prayer you can say is 'thank you,' that will be enough." I agree with him. Giving thanks connects us with all the people and events that have shaped our lives for the best. I make a point to say "thank you" to those who have helped me — or are helping me - on a daily basis. I also give thanks to the Source of all life, from whom we receive the gifts of life. I never run out of things for which to be thankful.

On this Thanksgiving, I'm especially thankful for you, Jack. I'm thankful that you're healthy and happy and have parents who love you, support you and raise you in a nice home and with good food. Grandma Kate and I are thankful that your dad is healthy. A few years ago, he was very sick. He had something called cancer, and spent three months getting treatments at the hospital to make him well. I'm thankful for the science that made it possible for you to be born. I'm thankful that we have a house large enough to have a big celebration where all the family can sit around the one big loving table. I'm thankful that we can gather as a family and enjoy organic turkey, potatoes, green beans, sweet potatoes, pumpkin pie, potatoes, cranberry sauce, wine, and all sorts of other good things. What a gift it is to sit beside the fire and share stories and enjoy each other's company. Your mom and Grandma Kate are putting together a jigsaw puzzle, one of their favorite things to do.

I'm thankful for the good work that I've been able to do as a writer, teacher, pastor, and seminary administrator. I'm thankful for my mom and dad – Loretta and Everett. You'll only know them by the few photographs I have of them and the stories I'll tell you about them, but they loved me and they loved your dad when he was a baby, and like your Grammy Max who loves you, they would have loved you if they were still living.

When you say "thank you," you're really remembering the abundant Spirit of Life that gives life to all things. We recognize that we didn't get here on our own, and that we can't grow without each other's help. Without our mother's milk and our daddy's arms, or someone else who cared for us, none of us would be here. I have decided to say "thanks" for every gift – for a friend or a colleague who calls me on the phone, for the person from whom I buy my groceries, for the police, fire, and military who protect us, for our government that builds roads and schools and cares for children whose parents don't have enough money. I pray for those who seek peace in the world and travel to far off countries to make sure children get enough to eat.

I hope you will always say "thank you," Jack, and do your best to help other people live good and healthy lives. Grandma and I try to pass our gratitude along by our commitment of time and talent to groups like Bread for the World, Church World Service, Amnesty International, and Susan B. Komen for the Cure. You'll discover that your gratitude comes back to you in feelings of joy for the simple gifts of life. That's what Thanksgiving is really about – giving thanks and doing good things for others, so they can give thanks along with you for the goodness of this wonderful life.

Love, Grandpa Bruce

WEEK FIFTEEN

BAPTISM

The Saturday after Thanksgiving, I gave you a special water blessing, Jack. Your grandparents – Bill, Cathy, and Kate – and your mom and dad were there. I said your name and added some words of thanks for your life and prayed that God would bless you with health, strength, and love. I prayed that you would always live in a loving home, surrounded by people who nurture you, bathe you in love, and help you learn what it means to live a good life, loving others as you love yourself. I asked your parents and grandparents to promise to teach you about love and generosity and care for others and help you grow spiritually all the days of your life, because these are the most important things in the world. Then, I sprinkled some drops of water on your head as a sign of your fresh new life and the love of God, friends, and family that constantly nourishes you.

You won't remember this day, Jack. You won't remember a lot of the most important things that happened this year – things that are the foundation for a trusting and loving life. We receive these gifts from the very beginning of our lives, before we can even say "thanks," and they're the seeds from which the rest of your life grows. But, hopefully, you will learn the meaning of baptism as you grow older.

Baptism is a very simple ritual. It involves a blessing on your life in which we wish good things for you and ask for a commitment from adults who love you to help you grow to love others. It's all about growth and relationship, with God, friends, and the world. Baptism is a special act that we do as Christians, but it also embraces every quest for health and growth and love. Important spiritual practices belong to everyone, not just one particular religion.

I believe that every child is blessed, whether she or he is a Jewish, Hindu, Muslim, First Nations, Buddhist, or raised by people who claim no religion. Some people call baptism a sacrament, which simply means to "make holy" or to "make love and grace come alive in this world." My prayer is that every moment of your life will be holy - special and beautiful – and that you will notice the beauty of others and bring it forth by your love. I pray that you will rejoice in the lively interdependence of life, from whom all blessings flow.

To me, baptism affirms that before you can do anything – when all you can do is eat and sleep and poop – you are loved unconditionally by the Spirit of Life, living and moving in all things. This Spirit joins us all, and enables us to lovingly reach out to others. You were welcomed into life with loving arms and those loving arms will guide and protect you throughout your childhood. I believe that baptism means that you are cherished by the Spirit of Life itself, what I choose to call God, simply because you are here. God loves you because of, and not in spite of, who you are! You belong here and have a right to grow. You were good and beautiful at the moment you were born, and you always will be!

The waters of baptism mean that your life is constantly refreshed with each new morning like a cool drink on a hot day. Baptism reminds us that the past is the springboard for the present and future and not a limitation on your gifts or creativity. You can begin again with every new day.

Often, when I take my morning shower, I imagine myself beginning again. I imagine myself letting go of past fears and limitations to embrace whatever new thing life demands of me today. As the day unfolds, I'm always surprised and grateful for all the new things that come my way.

Jack, someday I will share some more complex thoughts on baptism with you. But for now, just remember that through this "blessing of water" ceremony, those of us who were present promised to love, nurture, and protect. I take this seriously as I seek to love you with all my heart and protect you from any danger. Enjoy the energy of life and love flowing over and through you. That will be enough for you to live a good life now and in the years to come.

Love, Grandpa Bruce

WEEK SIXTEEN

DRESSING UP

When you're older and you look at your baby pictures, you'll be surprised at the outfits you wore in your first few months of life. It's plain to see that you're a fashionable young gentleman, Jack. Lions, tigers, monkeys, and dinosaurs adorn your shirts and pajamas. Bright stripes and polka dots shout out, "I'm here! Life is good! Let's play!"

Some of your outfits speak of the love your parents have for you: "Daddy's boy!" and "Mommy's boy!" and "I love you!" Some of your outfits are just cute, and announce to the world that your mom and dad are happy that you're their baby and want everyone to know how cute you are!

I think it's kind of neat that you wear lions and bears and tigers on your clothes. You're part of the animal kingdom, too. It's good to remember the beauty of animal babies and their own parents' love for them. Some of your favorite friends are animals – you have a lion, monkey, and elephant on your wall. We call them "Mr. Lion," "Mr. Monkey," and "Mr. Elephant." When we change your diaper, you reach out to them like they're your brothers and sisters. Maybe your animal-decorated clothes will help remind you to care for other animal friends when you're older.

It's good to dress up, Jack. Your dad likes to dress up, too. He likes to look sharp, neat, and well-groomed. It's a sign of self-affirmation. It says something to the world about who you are and that what you do really matters. It helps you stand out in the crowd as your own special self. But, the clothes don't make the man or the woman! There are all sorts of fashions that reflect who we are, our ethnic background, and what's important to us. Still, you can't judge people whose clothes are dirty or torn. It may mean that they don't have money to dress fashionably. We are all much more than our style and clothing. Beneath every person's clothes, there's a heart that beats and a soul that sings. We can dress up and delight in our clothing, but deeper than clothes is the beauty that's within you, Jack. You will keep growing taller and bigger for many years. You outgrow all your childhood clothes, but your spirit lives on through all the changes of life.

Differences are good, whether in your clothes, your ethnicity, your gender, or your religion. We need to celebrate all the colors of the rainbow – red, green, yellow, blue, and brown – and all the creatures of the earth, whether they walk, crawl, swim, or fly. It's good to dress up and rejoice in the wondrous variety of life. And, it's good to celebrate your own unique style and way of living. So, wear bright and bold colors, Jack, elephants and lions and sunshine faces. Have fun and enjoy the beauty, wonder, and diversity of all the people and creatures around you. Rejoice in the unity that joins us in all our diversity. We have hearts that beat and want to live and breathe and enjoy our lives on this good earth.

Love, Grandpa Bruce

WEEK SEVENTEEN

GOING TO THE DOCTOR

Today, your dad and I took you to the doctor. Now, although it's the first time your dad has taken you to the doctor, it's not the first time your dad has seen Dr. Idriss. One weekend, twenty five years ago, your dad had an ear infection. His regular pediatrician Dr. Guillermo Balfour was out of town. So, we took your dad to see Dr. Idriss, who was on-call that weekend. In the strange synchronicity of life, Dr. Idriss and his daughter (also Dr. Idriss) are now your doctors, Jack.

Going to the doctor – like a lot of things in life – isn't always fun. You like the novelty of going to the doctors' office and your two doctors are kind people. But none of us like the shots and the poking and prodding. When you go into the examination room, you're a little clingy and sometimes cry. Still, going to the doctor is a good thing. All of us need doctors and nurses to help us stay well and flourish in life. Going to the doctor is about taking care of yourself and trying to be as healthy as possible.

Your parents have done a good job in promoting your health. You drink lots of breast milk. They also insure that you live in a safe and warm house during the winter, and in the hot Washington DC summers, they will turn on the air conditioning to keep you cool. When you're older and can eat more solid food, your mom and dad plan to make most of your food – pureed organic fruits and vegetables. You're already going to yoga class to learn how to center, stretch, and bend, and start with good health habits that will last your whole of life.

When you're young, your health is your parents' responsibility. But when you get older, you'll make choices about what you eat and drink, and how much you exercise and sleep. Your health is a big deal and it involves a lot of things – your body, mind, spirit, emotions, and relationships. Everything about your life fits together and works together for health and wholeness.

I believe that what we eat shapes our moods and what we think and how we feel shapes our physical well-being. Do you know that when you're happy, you can feel good even if you have a cold? Do you know that when we love people, our cells light up and give us energy? They do! They literally glow with the light of the first day of creation.

When you meditate, your body rests and you feel calm and your mind becomes more creative. When you exercise, your mood becomes more positive and you get all sorts of new ideas. It's hard to hold on to old ideas when your body's in motion! Being touched with love makes you feel better and grow faster. So, I regularly give you a massage and place my hands on you in a way that brings healthy energy to your life. The technique I use is called reiki and it's a way sharing love by sharing healthy energy.[4]

When you get enough sleep, your whole body gets a chance to rest and relax and you have dreams that give you creative ideas and help you process what happened during the day. When we hug you, your whole body says "yes" and grows stronger and healthier.

So, take care of yourself, Jack. Eat well, sleep well, run around and play, love well, and enjoy your quiet times when you are alone for a nap or just to think about things. Let the healthy energies of life flow through you every day, so you can share your love with others.

Love, Grandpa Bruce

----

4 For more on reiki healing touch, see Bruce Epperly and Katherine Epperly, *Reiki Healing Touch and the Way of Jesus* (Kelowna, BC: Northstone, 2005).

WEEK EIGHTEEN

MERRY CHRISTMAS

When your dad was a young child, I read the Christmas stories from the Bible to him. Now, it's hard to explain what the Bible is, but for now, think of it as the story of people who wanted to know about how to live and how to love. It's about the relationship of people with the Creator of the Universe that we call God.

I wanted your Dad to know about the Baby Jesus and his parents Mary and Joseph. The Bible stories talk about Joseph as Jesus' father, but they also describe God as being Jesus' parent as well. The way that the Bible talks about the relationship of God and Jesus can be confusing to children as well as adults. People like me who spend their lifetimes thinking about God are called theologians and we have been trying to figure this out for two thousand years! After hearing the various stories of Jesus' birth, your dad asked me the following question: "If Joseph is Jesus' father, does that mean God is his grandfather?"

I think that your dad got the main point of those Christmas stories. Christmas is about relationships. It's about sharing joy as families and honoring the beautiful gifts of life. Christmas reminds us that the hope of the world comes with the birth of every child. Even in hard times, Christmas helps us feel hopeful because it's about love. This year we are hopeful because of your new little life!

We didn't have a white Christmas your first year. In fact, it was cold and dry. But a few days later your parents and you got caught in a big snow storm in New York City while you were visiting your mom's family. Regardless of the weather, we had fun being together. You spent hours gazing at the fire and soaking in the good feelings of hope, joy and love on Christmas Eve and Christmas morning when we opened presents.

For the first few years of your life, Christmas will mostly be about getting toys and playing with friends and family, and that's just fine. We want to give you great things and you'll receive all sorts of gifts from Grandma Cathy and Grandpa Bill and us. But in a few years, you'll also learn that Christmas is also about giving. We have received the gift of life and love, and we show our gratitude by being generous in giving to others as well as receiving. The more you give, the bigger your heart – your ability love and care for others - becomes and the happier you are. My heart is bigger because of you, little Jack.

You'll hear about angels and stars at Christmas. I'm no expert on angels, but the idea of spiritual beings who take care of us – special messengers of God's love in the world – helps us remember that we can be messengers of love, too. We don't need to be afraid because we are surrounded by light and love, and always have a star to guide us.

Right now, your baby's heart soaks up love – just like little Baby Jesus did from his mom and dad. The Baby Jesus needed to be fed and protected by his parents. He couldn't do anything but eat and sleep and poop when he was a little baby, just like you. But, he grew to be a great man because, first of all, his parents loved him. And, because he knew the love of his parents, he could tell people about God's great love. Today, his love is known around the world.

I believe that God is like a parent who loves everyone so much that he will search all day and even forever for each lost child. God will welcome us home even after we've run away and done things we regret.

Christmas is all about relationships. It's about the wonder and mystery of loving and living. It's about love that never begins and ends. And, it's about the love that creates the moon and stars and Mr. Lion and Mr. Monkey and Mr. Elephant! This is the sort of love your parents and grandparents have for you. May your baby's heart soak in all the love you can hold, so that someday you will become strong, generous and loving just like Jesus became when he grew up to be an adult. Then, everyday will be Christmas for you.

Love, Grandpa Bruce

WEEK NINETEEN

A BRAND NEW YEAR

Happy New Year's, Jack! It's snowing here in Lancaster and today I'm just going to sit by the fire, watch the Annual Tournament of Roses Parade from California, and invite your Uncle Bill, my brother, over for brunch.

I don't usually go to big parties on New Year's Eve. Grandma Kate and I usually spend a quiet evening with friends, sharing food, drink, and fellowship. We take time to remember the past year and imagine possibilities for the year ahead.

With the passing of the old year and the beginning of a new one, New Year's is a reminder that we can always begin again. But first we need to let go of the habits and hurts of the past. Right now, you're always "beginning" again, Jack, because you don't have a lot of habits and hurts. Every day is a new morning with brand new things to learn and experience. The past isn't a limitation for you as it is for many grownups. Yesterday holds the energy that pushes you forward to the next day's adventures. The adventures you have today help you grow into the possibilities that tomorrow will bring. But it doesn't always seem like that for grownups, so we have rituals to remind us.

New Year's reminds us that we are truly new every year and every morning. Life is a journey of growth and new life, whether or not we recognize it. Every moment of our lives is unique and unlike any other. Did you know that everything we do brings something new into the universe? It does! You will never have a day like today or a moment like right now. It is unique. It is yours

57

and yours alone. There is no room for boredom when every moment is a brand new opportunity for creativity and adventure.

There's a saying in a language called Latin that goes, "carpe diem." It means "seize the day." It means to claim each moment as part of a great adventure. That's what you're doing now, Jack. You are seizing each moment as something new, offering you new and bountiful possibilities for growing and learning and doing what you've never done before. Not much gets in your way! And, you're teaching me, Jack, to seize the opportunities of each day. You're helping me to remember that each moment can bring an "epiphany," a fancy word for saying that the lights go on in your heart and you see life with new eyes in all its amazing beauty and wonder.

Claiming the moment isn't always easy especially in challenging times. New Year's Day brings a big adventure for me. I just finished a job I held for nearly eight years and now I will be embarking on new adventures in my professional life. I will be seizing the moment as new things come my way.

This year I rejoice that life is new every morning. I will follow your example, Jack, and seize the wonder and beauty of this precious moment and the extra time I have to be with you. I will work hard to open my eyes to new possibilities as they emerge and let go of the limitations, hurts, and habits of the past as I embrace the wonders of the future as well as this present moment. Celebrate this amazing day! Happy New Year, Jack!

Love, Grandpa Bruce

WEEK TWENTY

SITTING UP

It's amazing how quickly you are growing, Jack. Recently, you've been sitting up on your own, though sometimes with the support of your "boppie" pillow. You are no longer relying on someone else's support to stay upright. You can sit up and roll a ball around all on your own! There are lots of milestones in a baby's first year, but sitting up is one of the most important ones. It is the prelude to standing, walking, and running, all of which you will be doing in the next six to nine months.

I know why you like to sit up, Jack. It makes you feel like a big boy. Even before you could sit up on your own, I propped you up on my lap or sat you right next to me on the couch whenever we read together. I know that you enjoyed holding the book in your hands, pointing and imitating the same things that I did when I read to you. For your age, you have a very good ability to focus and follow along when we're reading. You are slowly becoming more independent and able to do things yourself. Your world is getting bigger as you do more and more "big boy" things on your own.

We like to take pictures of you sitting up. I have a picture of your dad that I cherish. Your grandma took it and he's sitting up just like you, wearing a striped shirt and a sweater, and turning his head to look at the camera. It seems like yesterday, but it was nearly thirty years ago. Time passes – sometimes too quickly, it seems – and before we know it, you'll be walking and running. But, as time passes, there will always be special moments in your life and we need to celebrate them: your birthday, your first smile, sitting up for the first time, and later on crawling, walking, and running for the first time. I will hope you will join us in clapping your hands and feeling happy with each new "first."

Your circle of achievement will expand every day. The world is changing so fast. May you always keep growing and experience many more special moments as the years go by – first day of school, going to camp, sleeping over with friends, going to a foreign country, and falling in love for the first time, and yes – that, all important, "first" – driving your car.

I can hardly imagine what your life will be like in the next twenty years. These days, every nanosecond brings so many new developments in communications and global connections. But I'm sure that will be an adventure for you and for the rest of us.

Life truly is an adventure with surprises coming your way each day. Your life isn't planned out in advance. Lots of things – family, friends, and the world around you – will shape what you experience. Still you have choices to make, and you will shape who you will become by your choices every moment of the day. Whatever is going on in your life, you always have one freedom, the freedom to choose your attitude. This is the difference between being happy or unhappy, and being creative or bored. Your choices will shape other peoples' lives, and that is important too, as you always try to do the right thing.

Jack, may you always have an open and adventurous spirit like you do today. May you always be willing to do new things and go new places, and embrace the many "firsts" of our rapidly changing world.

Love, Grandpa Bruce

WEEK TWENTY-ONE

GRANDPA SNORES!

Even at five months, Jack, I can see that you have a fun-loving spirit. You're developing quite a sense of humor. Yesterday, your grandma reported the following incident to me. Of course, I can't verify it, because I was asleep! As your grandma tells it, I was napping on the sofa in the living room and all of sudden I began to snore. Now, not petite "excuse me" snores. But, real loud "send shock waves across the room" snores. You were sitting on your grandma's lap, reading a book. At first, it startled you. You stared at me and then you began to smile with your whole face. She said you laughed right out loud.

Now some things are just plain funny and I suspect a grown man making strange snoring noises when he's asleep is one of them. At least, I think it's funny, especially when someone else is snoring in public. But, I'll admit I can be funny, too, even when I'm asleep.

I'm so glad that you have a good sense of humor, Jack, because the ability to laugh at life – to recognize how silly life can be at times - is so important. The type of humor I'm talking about involves laughing with people and not at them, of course. Some people hurt others with their laughter. They make fun of people for the way they look, mistakes they make, or things they can't change – like their race, sex, intelligence, or speech patterns. But when you can laugh at strange and unexpected moments of life like a bad smell or a funny sound or watching your grandpa snoring, you have a chance to really enjoy life.

Remember not to take life too seriously. Some people say that angels can fly because they take themselves "lightly!" That's good advice. We need to take ourselves and others lightly, too. In your life, you will do important and difficult things, Jack. Sometimes you'll even see things that will break your heart. Bad things may even happen to you and those you love. But always look for the laughter and remember that "grandpa snores!" Let that help you to remember that in our lives joy and laughter, pain and sorrow, winning and losing, are all mixed together. But those who laugh will make it through life's tough times with health and hope for better days!

Love, Grandpa Bruce

WEEK TWENTY-TWO

CRYING

You're such a good-natured baby that my heart breaks whenever I hear you cry. Like your mom, dad, and grandma, I don't want you to ever feel unnecessary pain or experience being abandoned by the people you count on for food and love and touch. Some people believe that it builds maturity and character in children when we let them "cry it out" for several minutes at a time. I'm not so sure about this. I agree with Alice Walker's statement, "The most important question in the world is 'Why is this child crying?'"

I know that you cry for many reasons just like your dad did when he was a little boy. As your grandpa, I have to make a judgment call every time I hear you cry. This morning was no exception. I'm an early bird, so when I'm at your parents' house, I get up with you. As I read or meditate downstairs, I listen for sounds coming from your room.

This morning I heard you stirring at 4:00 a.m. That's even early for me, and, as I said, I'm an early riser. So, I waited. You cried a moment or two and then you went back to sleep. Sometimes, when a baby cries, an adult just has to listen to make sure everything's alright. Two hours later, after you fussed for a few minutes, I went in and we began the day together – on a happy note. Your cry was an announcement to the world: "I'm up. I'm alone. I want someone to be with. Let's do something together." Now, that's reason enough to respond.

Sometimes you cry when you're hungry and, then, a breast or a bottle will do the trick. Other times you cry when you're getting a new tooth. That's happening a lot these days. We give you something to chew on or a little medication to soothe the pain, and in a few minutes you feel better.

Some tears are inevitable in life. Your tears are part of expressing your needs before you have words to communicate what you want. But no one needs to cry longer than necessary – that's why we have medicine and loving arms.

Now there are people who see crying always as a way of getting what you want. They use a big and serious word, "manipulation," to describe the way babies get adults to do things by their tears. Now, I'm not sure about this. I don't think babies manipulate in their first few months of life. But I do think they express what they need, and try to find people who will respond. That's just life. It's a rhythm of call and response, and learning who is most likely to help us get what we need at the moment. We need to tell people what we need. If we don't ask, we won't receive. But we also need to be alert to what the people around us need as well.

Later on, I think some babies – and even adults – use tears to make other people feel guilty or do what they want, but that's a behavior they learn because it's the only way, in some families, they can get attention, or because they don't have enough words yet.

I want to tell you something, Jack, and I'm fast forwarding about six months to your first birthday. Sometimes you cry to get what you want right now, and I can tell. So, I cry with you, mirroring you, and you stop crying. Sometimes you won't get what you want and you'll want to cry just to get your way, but it's better to talk it out with other people and find a way to get your needs met, and help others get their needs met, too. When you are older, you'll learn signs and words to communicate.

64

You'll discover that most of the time, talk is better than tears when you need something.

As you get older, Jack, there will be times when we'll let you cry a few minutes before we respond. Other times, we'll say something like, "It's time to go to bed" and hold you when you thrash about, feeling tired but unable to sleep. We may even put you in your crib and let you cry a few minutes just to see if you can go to sleep on your own. What we're trying to do is help you begin to make decisions about your sleeping and waking. We're also trying to gently teach you that, while you are the center of *your* universe, you aren't the only center of *the* universe.

The Center of Life is really everywhere and in everyone. Everyone matters, not just you and me. Sometimes other peoples' needs are more pressing – or important than yours – at a particular moment and you will learn to be patient until it's your turn.

So, Jack, we take your crying seriously. We listen well to try to figure out what's bothering you and then we try to respond in the most loving way – that soothes and reassures you, but also helps you grow to be a big boy.

It's good to cry sometimes. Later on, your cries will take on a new form. You'll learn how to communicate your needs in a world where other people have needs. You'll begin to use words like, "I'm hungry," "I want you to lie down with me," "I want a hug," "I'm afraid and I want someone with me," "I feel sad." And, you can count on us to respond. We may even share our "cries" with you: "I'll be with you in a minute. Let me finish this project," "I feel bad today, too," or "I really want to be with you, but I have to go to work."

There are times when you'll cry when you're very sad. When you see somebody that's hurt or feeling bad, or discover the pain of the world. That's when I cry, and then it's good to let your emotions show. It's good to share how you feel, especially to the people you trust to care for you. Sometimes when you share how you feel and someone responds to you, you discover that even if you have to wait awhile, you can take care of yourself and be patient until you see that familiar and loving face.

Love, Grandpa Bruce

WEEK TWENTY-THREE

COUNTING TO TEN

Early on, we discovered that you like numbers. You pay attention when we say "one, two, three," "uno, dos, tres," or "un, deux, trois." Even though, you don't exactly know what these words mean, you stop what you're doing whenever someone says "one duck, two ducks" or "one, two, three teeth," or "uno, dos, tres gatos" [cats]. I think you like the pattern of the words and their sense of connection with one another.

Numbers are important. They help us keep track of things. In the years to come, you'll learn how patterns of numbers operate cell phones, computers, and clocks. But, these days, we've discovered another good purpose for numbers. They help you be patient.

Now, patience is a difficult virtue for both adults and babies. I think that I'm a pretty patient person. But, when I have to wait thirty seconds to get my e-mail, I begin to tap my feet impatiently. I don't like slow computers! When you go to the store, you see people get impatient and angry if they have to wait in line for a few minutes. Even babies get impatient! Even, you, Jack get impatient when you want something right NOW!

When you're impatient, Jack, sometimes you start to cry or give out a little protest squeal. Right now, the things that make you impatient are having to wait to eat, getting bored playing by yourself, getting tired of a book or a toy you've been playing with, or not getting Mom, Dad, Grandpa, or Grandpa to get you out of bed quick enough when you wake up.

I've begun playing a game with you to help you become more patient. Whenever you begin to cry at the dinner table, I say, "Let's count to ten." And so I count really slowly, "one… two…three…four…five…six….seven….eight…nine….ten." Like magic, you calm down until your dinner is on the table.

Now I've discovered an interesting way to deal with my impatience at the computer. While I'm waiting for my mail to come up, I take a deep breath and say a little prayer – for you, for your grandma, for your mom and dad, for my best friends, and for the world. Then, I forget my impatience. You could say that we are distracting you when we count to ten and I'm distracting myself when I pray. But maybe what we're trying to do is to change how we look at time, moving from focusing on just this moment and what we want right now to seeing our lives in a larger framework. I think it's about perspective and discovering that we have more time than we thought. We don't need to be impatient. We don't need everything right this very moment. We can just enjoy listening to the numbers, breathing deeply, or praying for those we love. We always have enough time for the important things, so why hurry when this moment has everything we need to be happy? "Uno…dos…tres…quatro…cinco… seis…siete…ocho…. nueve…diez."

Love, Grandpa Bruce

WEEK TWENTY-FOUR

BIG BOY JACK!

You are nearly six months old, Jack, and everything in you wants to crawl! When you get up and read with me each morning, you start pumping your legs, up and down and up and down, like a piston, ready to roar off for a race. Deep down, we're always growing even when we don't notice it. The forward movement of life is drawing you to the next adventure – creeping, crawling, walking, and running. And, you're ready to go!

Every day your dad calls to you: "Big boy, Jackie, Jackie! Big boy, Jackie, Jackie!" Your face becomes one great grin and then you move into action, jumping up and down, crawling while you're standing still.

Big boy, Jack! Nature wants you to think big. Life wants you to dream big and then live your dreams.

The most important things in life happen when you think big. When he was a baby, Dr. Helder, your dad's pediatrician in Mount Pleasant, Michigan, told us that he'd be 6'2" when he grew up. Even though he was a small boy, we told him, "Someday, you're going to be a big man. You'll be taller than Mom and Dad. You're going to be 6'2". Over the years, your dad saw himself as becoming a tall man, and today, your dad is 6'2". He became the person he imagined that he'd become. Life was bursting forth inch by inch, but just maybe his dreams helped him grow.

Now we don't know how tall you'll become in the years ahead. Right now, you're pretty small – 25th percentile in weight and height, with a 10th percentile head size. But, to us, you are just right. Nothing could be better than the way you are today. Your head and body couldn't be more perfect – they belong together!

Still, think big and dream big. Always see yourself as doing more than you can imagine. Always see yourself as strong, brave, and bright, able to do great things for the world. As a matter of fact, right now, you're doing great things. You've hatched the dream of a crawling boy and, before you know it, you're going to be walking. I think that when you move your legs up and down, in your mind, you're already running, not baby steps but big steps toward the future.

Believe it or not, some adults quit dreaming. They forget that as infants and toddlers they had big dreams. They forget that deep down the forces of life want them to move forward to new horizons and bigger possibilities. They let their imaginations shrink to the limits of the present moment. They no longer expect great things of themselves or the world. They can't visualize life being different than it is today, regardless of how bad things are.

But the great women and men of the world – like crawling babies – dream big. A great American, Martin Luther King, had a dream, and it was a big dream – about a country where people of all colors walked hand in hand as fellow Americans, who honored and affirmed each other despite of their differences. There's a statue of Dr. King in the Mall in your hometown, Washington DC. Someday we'll go to see it. There are monuments to other great dreamers – Abraham Lincoln, Thomas Jefferson, and George Washington. When you're older, I intend to tell you about people who had big dreams and did great things – people like Helen Keller, Mother Teresa, Albert Einstein, Mahatma

Gandhi, Nelson Mandela, Barack Obama – that changed the world.

I'll tell you about Jesus of Nazareth, who had a vision of beauty in places of ugliness, healing in places of sickness, and goodness in places of evil. He saw each person as bigger than they imagined and invited them to stand up, walk, and change the world.

You will do great things, Jack, even if no one notices. If you think bigger than you are, and dream great dreams about yourself and the world, every day will be filled with excitement, growth, and adventure.

Love, Grandpa Bruce

WEEK TWENTY-FIVE

REMEMBERING GRANDPA

I didn't feel hurt, but I felt bad that you were scared. I'd been away for a week, but when I came through the door and reached out to give you a big hug, you started crying. It seemed like you were saying: "Who is this stranger who's just picked me up?" Everything was lovey-dovey last week and now you don't even remember me, Jack.

Well, I should have realized that your mental soft wiring is still in process, Jack. You're constantly learning new things – almost more than an adult like me can imagine – and you can't be expected to hold everything in your mind all the time.

After a minute or two, you remembered me. A big smile broke out on your face as if to say, "I remember you. You're one of the people who holds me, feeds me, and makes me feel safe and secure."

Forgetting isn't a bad thing. We seem to forget for a lot of reasons. When we're getting started in life, we're just trying to make sense of the chaos of life: we're trying to understand all the different sounds, colors, smells, tastes, and textures. It's really a lot to take in, especially when every day seems like a whole new beginning.

When we're older, sometimes we forget for the same reason. Life is just too much for us. There are so many things happening, and they seem to come all at once. I have ten different passwords to remember for my computer, e-mail, Facebook, Twitter, work, ATM, and business accounts, and sometimes I get them confused. There's just too much information to process. When we're even older, we forget as part of the aging process. Even brains can get tired and may not work the way they used, too.

But now, you're learning so many things. Your brain is agile and open to everything. Anything can be interesting and a source of new information. You're reaching out to the world without limits on what you can learn and who you can become.

Later on, Jack, you'll remember me every time I visit. You'll run up to me shouting, "Grandpa!" and you'll have that same beautiful smile on your face. When I call you on the phone, you'll remember my voice and we'll talk about all sorts of things. I will be the happiest grandpa because we'll be learning new things together every day, and we will remember the important things – to love, to help, and to learn.

Love, Grandpa Bruce

WEEK TWENTY-SIX

TAKING A BOTTLE

For most of your first six months, Jack, you've been breast-fed. Breast feeding is good; it bonds you and your mother, it's natural and nutritious, and can prevent certain allergies. Right now, it all comes through your mother's milk.

After six months at home with you, your mom's going back to work. So, recently, you've been taking a bottle so you'll have plenty eat when your mother's gone. Your mom and dad are giving you an organic formula to supplement your mom's milk and respond to your ever growing hunger. You're growing a lot these days, Jack, and growth requires lots of good healthy food.

You didn't like the bottle at first. It was strange and it wasn't mother. But now you look forward to it. There are good reasons to take a bottle. Drinking from a bottle is your first step to enjoy-ing the wonderful world of food. In the next few months, you'll be sampling apple sauce, pears, beans, oatmeal, and salmon. Then, later, you'll discover your favorite foods. I suspect that you will be a gourmet, Jack, like your dad. You'll be someone who appreciates a good meal, with subtle spices and aromas. You'll enjoy casual and unhurried conversation around the din-ner table and you'll relax in front of the TV with grandma and grandpa and a big bowl of popcorn.

Your father and I enjoy food. I love Tex-Mex, exotic cheeses, tuna steaks, and a good piece of pie. Of course, I like good strong coffee and milk shakes, too! We Epperly men have a taste for the good life, and so will you.

74

But right now, you're sitting in my arms, enjoying a bottle looking up at me with eyes of love as you prepare to drift off to sleep. That bottle is about bonding with the people who love you. In the circle of life, it begins with your mom, the source of all nourishment and nurture. But then you'll discover that your dad loves you just as much, and you'll know it because he holds you and changes your diaper and plays with you and feeds you. Grandma and I love to give you the bottle, too, because it's one of the many ways we show our love.

Yes, Jack, there's a whole world of food out there. I hope food will always be a joy to you, not too much, but just enough for good health and joyful celebration. I hope that you'll always remember that some babies don't have enough food – these babies can't even find a breast or a bottle to drink from. Right now your dad is working to find ways for children in Somalia, a country in Africa, to get more food. When you're older, if there are still hungry children, remember the children of those babies and make sure that they get good food, too. That's the best way to say thanks for everything you received from your parents when you were small.

Love, Grandpa Bruce

WEEK TWENTY-SEVEN

TEETHING

No one likes pain. Some pain is bad, but pain can also be part of growth. The problem is that we sometimes don't know the difference between good pain and bad pain. When you were born, your mom experienced the pain of childbirth, but she also experienced great joy, because she knew that it meant you'd be coming soon.

Sometimes pain is part of getting better when we're sick. When your dad was diagnosed with cancer, he received certain chemicals – it's called chemotherapy. They made him feel sick at times, but they helped cure the cancer. You're here because of a man named Larry Einhorn who created the medical treatment that saved your dad's life.

But teething - that just hurts! It keeps you awake. It makes you cranky. And, sometimes you even cry because you don't know why it hurts. It just hurts! I don't want to underestimate your pain; but teething is good pain. Teething is a sign that you're growing, getting good nourishment, and new teeth are on the way.

Right now, all you eat is breast milk and a little formula. When you get teeth, you'll be able to eat all kinds of food – salmon and beans, crackers and cheerios, carrots and apples, cheese and avocados, and pasta and nachos. You'll discover new flavors and all the good food you can eat. Take a look at your grandpa. I'm proof that there's lots of good food around!

Still, you can't deny it, teething hurts. There's nothing you can do to avoid it, except maybe a medication that eases the pain or a cloth or cracker to suck on. For the next year or so, you'll feel teething pain every so often. But oh the joy of a new tooth breaking through and then another and another. It's all part of the human adventure – of getting bigger, learning new things, and sampling the delicacies of this good earth.

There are times when pain can be good, Jack. It can be a sign of growth. A little pain can be your muscles' response to beginning an exercise program. It can be your response to new ideas that force you to change the way you look at the world. And it can be a warning that something is wrong and that you need to see a doctor. No one likes pain, but without some types of pain, there wouldn't be any growth and you wouldn't be able to know you're in danger. So, take your teething in stride, Jack, and know that someday you'll be eating an apple or chewing a carrot, thankful for all those teeth!

Love, Grandpa Bruce

WEEK TWENTY-EIGHT

MOMMY'S AT WORK

You're a lucky guy, Jack. Your mom was able to stay home nearly seven months with you. This is a great blessing. It provided security and bonding, and great opportunities for breast feeding and feeling at home in the universe. At the beginning of your life, your mom is the universe. She is the window through which you see the world and the source of health and nourishment. Your world has grown wider over the past seven months. You have met new people and have gotten to know your dad and grandparents as people you can trust to take care of you.

Now, something new has come into your life. Your mom is going back to work. She is an attorney and she will be working hard at the office. But she and your dad have made sure that you're taken care of. Monday to Wednesday, Maria will be your caregiver. She is a lovely person with a big heart and I know she loves you and will do anything to make sure your life is healthy and safe. Your Grandma Kate is coming down on Thursdays and Fridays, because she loves you and wants to make sure that you're healthy and safe. She's really playful and a good teacher. She will help you learn words and shapes and all sorts of games. I know you'll have fun with her.

There's a bonus for me, too. I'll be coming down to visit nearly every week also. I'll be your early morning man. We both get up early and morning will be our play time. We'll read books and listen to music and walk around the neighborhood long before your mom, dad, and grandma are awake.

I feel blessed that I don't have an office to go to these days. I'm working for myself giving talks and leading seminars. I love the work I'm doing and it gives me a lot of free time to see you. I didn't want to leave my job at first. I loved my work at the Seminary. But now I consider it a blessing that in the first year of your life, I can spend a lot of time just loving you and growing with you. Sometimes, things you didn't want to happen to you, like a job change, end up turning out for the best. Some people call that the dark cloud that hides silver lining. Others call it God's grace amid life's challenges. I'm grateful for this grace time to get to know you. I may go back to work at another school next year, but I'm savoring the freedom of being with you, and in this very moment!

I know that you'll be missing Mom. She will be missing you as well. But this is the beginning of a great circle of growth for you and the family. You'll learn that there will always be someone to love you and provide for your needs. Because people love you and care for you today, someday, little Jack, you'll grow up to be a man who can be depended on to care for others just like your mom and dad care for you.

Love, Grandpa Bruce

WEEK TWENTY-NINE

CRAWLING BACKWARD

Each time I see you, I'm amazed at how much you've grown. It's just been four days since the last time, and you are doing all sorts of new things! My practice has been to come down for two days each week to help your parents out and watch over you while they go out to shop or have some time together. For your grandma and me, seeing you is one of the greatest joys of our lives.

This week you started crawling, but you were crawling backwards. You'd push yourself – with your strong arms – and then surge backwards sometimes in a circle around the toys with which you were playing. Now pediatricians have an explanation for why most babies crawl backward at first; their arms are simply stronger than their legs.

But I was amazed this week, first, that out of the blue you started crawling. No one told you to. No one pushed you into it. One day, everything fitted together and off you went – in reverse!

I think there's an inner spirit that inspires each step of your – and, given the proper conditions, every baby's - growth. Without thinking you learned to latch and suck from your mother's breast. Without any forethought, you began to play at rolling over. Without too much urging, you began to try to sit up straight and then you did. Now you are being propelled by a gentle inner energy to crawl and soon to walk.

You are crawling in reverse and that's amazing too! You have to crawl backward to move forward. You have to reverse direction to find the toys that are right in front of you.

Sometimes you crawl backward in circles, ending at the place you began.

I think it's a good thing to move forward by going backward. Sometimes we need to slowly investigate where we are before we take action. Moving forward too quickly might keep us from discovering the wonders that are right beside us. While I don't crawl backward very often these days, your backward crawl has taught me a very important lesson. I try to begin each day taking time to meditate. Meditation is a way of crawling backward to go forward. When I meditate, I retreat from the busyness of life. Fifteen or twenty minutes in the morning help me go forward with wisdom the rest of the day. Sometimes when I'm writing or working on a problem, I have to go into reverse to see the chain of thoughts or actions that I need to consider before moving ahead with my work.

Don't ever worry about going backward and taking time to be still and rest. Going backward, finding a quiet and safe place, can help you go forward with energy on your next adventure.

Love, Grandpa Bruce

WEEK THIRTY

YOUR BIG BOY VOICE

For the past few weeks, you've been greeting each day with conversation. You've been clicking your tongue, going "ooh" and "aaah" and "bababa" and "dadada" and sharing all sorts of ideas. I don't always understand you, but I know you are saying something really important. I try to mirror your words with my own, as we go back and forth in a "call and response" while we're playing with toys or watching *Dinosaur Train* on PBS. It gives you great pleasure to share your story and have someone respond with their own words or a version of your words.

It's more than just baby talk. It's about making a connection and sharing how you feel. Communicating is one of the most important things in the world, even for something simple like "I need a bottle" or "I hurt" or "I'm happy."

Today you discovered your big voice and fell in love with it. You raised your voice an octave, squealing and shouting to the rafters. It was clear that you enjoyed the sound of your own voice. But you were even happier when one of the adults mimicked you, squealing with you in harmony. Father and son, grandfather and grandson, singing in harmony, for the pure joy of it!

Although there will be times you'll need to be quiet or speak softly, it is simply wonderful to have a big voice! So many people are afraid to express how they feel. Other people aren't heard – no one seems to listen because they're different or sing out of tune. Some people never learn that their voice matters and is beautiful just the way it is. But not you, Jack! Your winsome smile warms the room and your cry says "I'm hungry and I want to be fed" or "I'm awake and want to play."

Some days you literally sing yourself awake. It's almost like you want to be in tune with the songbirds outside, making their own joyful noise. A song on one of your CD's says, "Sing your song." I hope you always have a song to sing and the courage and creativity to sing your own particular melody just for the pure joy of it! When you're older, I hope you listen to other people's songs, especially the songs of those who are forgotten or neglected, and help them find their voices, too. So sing your song, loud and strong, all the day long.

Love, Grandpa Bruce

THIRTY-ONE

UNCLE BILL

You met my brother Bill twice at my home in Lancaster. He loved little things – like his cat – and he loved you. When he heard you had been born, he called all his friends and told all his neighbors in the mobile home park where he lived. He was especially proud of your name, "Jack Everett," because his name was "William Everett."

Sadly, Jack, your Uncle Bill will only be a photo and name for you. You see, my brother died just the other day, March 28. Now, death is hard to explain at any age. For a few more years, you won't have a sense of what it means for a person to leave and never return. There is no hurry in knowing about death, Jack. There is enough loss in life without having to deal with the big ones – like war and death - when you're just a little boy.

But I want to tell you a little bit about my brother Bill. He was three years older than me. His life was difficult; he never really had a job and lived with his parents most of his life. He was a little boy in a giant's body. Emotionally, he never grew up. He was always anxious, sometimes heard voices that weren't there, and lived in a fantasy world. He felt panic when he was in public places like stores and restaurants. But he was my brother and though we had our problems, I loved him. I did my best to take care of him just like I take care of you.

Several years ago, I bought a mobile home for him and then moved him from California to Lancaster, Pennsylvania, just a few miles from our home. At first, it was tough for him to be in a new place, but he grew to love the family dinners, football games, and the changing seasons.

Now, my brother never accomplished much in the eyes of the world. But everyone can be a hero in the course of her or his life. My brother was a hero by just getting out of bed and going to the store, despite all his fears. My brother Bill was a hero when I was five years old. Mean old Mrs. Andrus, the kindergarten teacher, frightened all her students. She was a sour puss. For some reason, she kept me after school one day. I can't imagine why, but like you, Jack, I may have smiled too much!

My brother's task that day was to walk me home and no one was going to stop him. When Mrs. Andrus told Bill that I had to stay after school, he got mad and then he acted. He took my hand and walked me out of the classroom. He told Mrs. Andrus that "my parents wanted me home," and that was that, regardless of what the teacher thought.

I always remembered that time, and so did Bill. He had that one shining moment when he did something great to help out his little brother. As one of our favorite songs says, "Every little soul must shine, must shine."

Right now, Jack you are open hearted toward everyone. You will grow in insight and street smarts, but always remember that a light shines within everyone, and even when it seems to be disguised, it's still there. The inner beauty and wonder of life shined through my brother – your Uncle Bill – and it shines through all of God's children. So, look for the light in all its hidden places. There is a hero inside you, Jack, and everyone else. "Love brought us here," as the song says, and love brings out the light and heroism in all of us.

Love, Grandpa Bruce

THIRTY-TWO

PELIGRO

Babies are curious creatures. Because you're a bright young fellow, Jack, you are more curious than most. You're interested in everything, especially what we don't want you to get into. Lots of things that are safe when you're older can be dangerous when you're a baby or toddler. Your mom and dad baby-proofed the house, put up baby gates, and placed things like knives and computers out of reach. But, those are the things that interest you. Those are the things you want to touch and hold and play with.

When your dad was a little boy, Grandma and I used the word "peligro," a Spanish word that means "danger," whenever he got near the wood stove or oven. We've revived the word "peligro" to let you know when you're too close to something dangerous. Today, I think we said it twenty times as you reached for cords, fans, and glasses.

Danger can be a magnet for children and even adults. What's forbidden can become all the more attractive. Frankly, what you hear from those who know better isn't always convincing when you just want to touch the flame or play with your parents' computer keyboard. I don't blame you, Jack, for pushing the limits. Curiosity is essential to learning, but curiosity will take you places where adults and other authority figures don't want you to go and sometimes those places are full of danger. The key is somehow to figure out the difference between risks that are worth it and those who aren't.

But for now, it's important to trust Mom and Dad even when you want to push the limits. They always have your best interests in mind. Believe it or not, as you get older, some things that are dangerous now – like turning on the stove, cutting with a knife, or climbing up the stairs – will become routine. New things will become dangerous – like drugs, alcohol, driving when you're tired, and walking in tough neighborhoods. In the years ahead, you'll hear variations of the word "peligro" time after time from authority figures, and you'll keep pushing the limit – especially when you're a teenager - as you try to figure out the difference between healthy curiosity and risky business.

What I've found best is that when you're not sure, don't do it. When the voice inside says "no," trust it. Know that you can always come to me for advice. I love you and will always share my wisdom – I pushed the limits too and so did your dad when he was younger – and somehow we both survived. Still, remember that some things are really dangerous, so play it safe, even when you're on an adventure.

Love, Grandpa Bruce

WEEK THIRTY-THREE

A BABE MAGNET AT
APPALACHIAN SPRING

This afternoon the two of us went on an errand to Appalachian Spring, a store highlighting artists from Appalachia, to pick up a necklace your mom had repaired. It was a glorious day in Georgetown and we reveled in the Washington DC spring as you sped down Wisconsin Avenue in your "hot rod" stroller.

But, the real fun began when we picked up the jewelry. Five women, between twenty five and fifty five surrounded you, and were each vying for your attention. Of course, you reciprocated, giving each one of them your brightest, most alluring and flirtatious smile. You sure liked the attention and although you didn't understand the words, you got the message – they thought you were something special! And you are!

Now, Jack, it was good to bask in your glory. I didn't feel too bad because they were paying attention to me, too. Even your grandpa likes the attention of women!

I don't know if there's any moral lesson to be learned here, Jack, except to receive the good wishes of others with gratitude and humility. There's a good chance that you'll always be a magnet to men and women, and with that comes the responsibility to always be worthy of their adoration. This means that you aim not only to be a good looking young man, but more importantly a good man, who treats women and men with respect, and who brings out the best in the people who care for you.

While looking good is important, having a beautiful soul is the most important thing in the world. This is the beauty that endures forever. It will bring joy and love to everyone you meet.

This is the magnetism that really matters. It joins your heart with others and expands the circle of love and care, so that everyone around you knows that they're beautiful too. One more thing, always remember that you are beautiful, even if no one notices you.

Love, Grandpa Bruce

WEEK THIRTY-FOUR

WHAT A MORNING!

We are morning persons, you and me. When I was a little boy, I woke up at 6:00 a.m. every morning to spend time with my dad. We read books and ate breakfast before my brother and mother got up. Your dad and I had the same practice: when your dad was a little boy, we read books, ate breakfast, and then played catch or kick ball in the back yard until it was time to go to school. Grandma Kate always sleeps in, so your dad and I had lots of time to play and read.

Morning is the best time of day for me. When I'm home in Lancaster, I wake up about 4:45 a.m., meditate, and then take a three mile walk in the hills around our home. Then I come home and write for an hour or two.

But, when I'm with you, Jack, I let go of my daily routine, because you're a morning person, too. It's our time, Grandpa and Baby Jack having fun together. But what a morning it was today! I heard you stirring before 5:00 a.m. That's early even for you. After hearing you talk to yourself in your crib for a few minutes, I came in and was greeted by the most beautiful smile in the world. Your smile can light up the room and warm your grandpa's heart.

This morning, we went out on the front steps and just listened and watched. The birds were singing melodies as intricate as Bach, Beethoven, the Beatles, and the Beach Boys. The North African monks – people who devoted their lives to knowing God – believed that a monk should be "all eye" in his attention to the intricate beauties of life. Well, this morning, you were all eyes and all ears, taking in the wonder of it all.

A Jewish teacher, Abraham Joshua Heschel, said that the heart of religion is the experience of radical amazement. If that's so, then babies like you can be spiritual teachers, Jack. You were totally in the here and now, reveling in the wonder of being awake at sunrise. Life was amazing in its wonder and beauty.

Some people begin the day in a foul mood. They just don't want to get out of bed, and feel grumpy all the way through the morning. But, Jack, doesn't it feel good to wake up ready for adventure, peering out of your crib poised to see something beautiful and do something you've never done before?

Sadly, many grownup people and even some children lose the sense that each day is a gift and adventure. But, we revel in the joy of each new day. There will never ever be a morning like this one, Jack, and tomorrow brings a new morning and you can wake up with joy, wondering what new and surprising thing will happen just because you woke up today! So, my dear grandson, let's celebrate and rejoice in this wonderful day!

Love, Grandpa Bruce

WEEK THIRTY-FIVE

A WILL OF YOUR OWN

This morning, Jack, you showed that you not only have a big voice, but a big will, too! After we strolled through Georgetown, we sat down on a bench and you sat on my lap for a few minutes, observing the sights and sounds of Georgetown University. You turned this way and that to see the students walking by and get a closer look at the flowers beside our bench. But when I tried to put you back in the stroller, you let me know what you thought about that idea. You squirmed and straightened out like a board to keep me from putting you in. I waited for a moment or two, asked you to get back in the stroller, and eventually you let me strap you in for a happy and safe ride home.

Now, it's a good thing to have a will of your own and to like certain things and dislike others. That's built into who we are. As you grow older, you'll discover more and more things that you like and dislike, and you'll want to let the significant people your life know your preferences. That's what communication is all about.

It is a good thing to know what you want, Jack. But one of the things you discovered this morning is that I have a will, too. Sometimes, it's good to pay attention to what others want. This morning, I was happy to carry you for a block or so to accommodate your will. But I knew it would be difficult to carry you five blocks home and roll the stroller, too. There was a reason for my challenging your will and eventually putting you back in the stroller.

It will take awhile, but eventually you will realize that you'll be happier when you can find a way to balance what you want with the reasonable desires of other people – first of all your parents and grandparents, and Maria your nanny, and later other children and adults. You will discover that you can present options to those who have different ideas. You can ask them what they need, and you can find ways for everyone to get what they need.

Still, don't ever hide what you want, especially from yourself. Listen to your heart, and follow your dreams. There are a lot of adults who have quit wanting things. They just try to fit in and not make waves. Still, it's important to know what you want, and then find ways of deciding if what you want is good for you and for those around you. I'm happy that you are having a growing sense of your likes and dislikes and learning to tell us what you want. If you can't say "yes" to what you want, you won't be able to say "no" to some very bad things – like drugs and alcohol or going along with friends who want to do things that will hurt you and others. And, if you can't say "no" and assert your feelings and needs, you won't be able to say "yes" and stand by your "yes" to big commitments like helping your mom and dad around the house, volunteering at a soup kitchen, standing by someone who's being picked on, or becoming good at art or writing or playing baseball.

This morning, it was good for you to resist my will, and I liked your push back when I wanted to put you in the stroller. But it was also good to see you cooperate and realize that the best way to get home was to follow my lead and ride in the stroller. Sometimes we can find a meeting of the wills and we can do great things together.

Love, Grandpa Bruce

WEEK THIRTY-SIX

WITH A TILT OF THE HEAD
YOU GET A NEW PERSPECTIVE
ON LIFE

For the past few weeks, I've observed you doing something really wonderful. Whenever you want to see something from another your angle, you tilt your head. Sometimes you almost slip off my lap or fall out of your chair – you tilt yourself so far to one side or the other. Now, this is a big deal – to see things from a new perspective.

When you're a little older, I'll get you a kaleidoscope. A kaleidoscope is a circle of mirrors, almost like a telescope, with beads or colorful pieces of glass inside. Whenever you turn it, the whole scene changes, with new patterns constantly being created and recreated.

Looking at things from different perspectives is essential to living a good life. As you grow older, you'll discover some people who can only look at things one way. They believe that there's only one way to do things or only one right answer to every question. If you have a different idea, they'll tell you that they're right and you're wrong. They won't compromise on the "truth" as they understand it or grow when new ideas are presented to them.

Some people still think the earth is the center of the universe, God only loves people like them, and humans have only existed eight thousand years. They reject the evidence of science whenever it challenges their beliefs. They forget that we live in a grand universe with more stars and galaxies than any of us can imagine. A different perspective helps you see that goodness and truth can come from anyone and any group. I have discovered there is often more than one right answer to life's most important questions.

You're already learning, Jack, that you can look at the same thing from different angles and discover new things every time you look at it. Today, you were looking at my face, first from one side and then the other. First, you focused on my chin, then my beard, and mouth. Then, you examined my eyes and hair. I could tell that this was infinitely interesting to you. With each look, you saw something new. I'm not the only interesting thing in your world. You can spend several minutes tilting your head this way and that as you look at a toy car or stuffed toy.

That's a good way to look at life, Jack. There's always more than meets the eye, and sometimes more than one answer to the same question. You can enjoy different perspectives on life, knowing that there's always more to learn about everything you look at. Just shift your attention and you'll discover new ways to understand a problem or find something interesting in someone you've just met. You may even learn to see the world from another point of view – from that of an older person, or a person of a different race or gender or country. You will grow and become a more sensitive and caring person because you'll keep tilting your head to see life from a different perspective.

Love, Grandpa Bruce

WEEK THIRTY-SEVEN

PEEKABOO

This morning you and Grandma discovered a new game. Grandma covered you with a blanket and then lifted the blanket as she exclaimed, "Peek-a-boo!" You smiled and laughed with the joy of discovery. For a moment, Grandma disappeared and then in the blink of an eye, she appeared again.

Now peek-a-boo is a pretty simple game, but it tells us something that's necessary for a happy life. Even when we don't see something, it may still be there. People and toys still exist even when you can't see them. That's a big lesson, Jack, because it helps us trust that we'll be okay when the people we love are in the other room or go to work.

These days, you're learning this lesson almost every morning. When you wake up, you're all alone in your room. Mom and Dad are usually sleeping across the hall. Sometimes they're still fast asleep as you crawl around your crib or lean against the sides, first, talking to yourself and then calling out after a few minutes to the Most Important People in the World, Mom and Dad, or Grandma and Grandpa, the people who will greet you with a smile and start the day off with a hug and diaper change.

Life is constantly changing, and for you, Jack, each day is a unique opportunity to go on new adventures and learn new skills. In simple games like peek-a-boo or rolling a ball on the rug, you are creating the soft-wiring for everything you'll learn in the future.

We need lots of changes for life to stay interesting. Without change – without new things happening – we won't grow and life will eventually become boring. But we also need something dependable to count on. We need to know that when we close our eyes at night that there's a world that keeps on going and the people that you love and need are here for you regardless of all the changes you experience.

You don't have words yet to describe this rhythm of change and stability, and presence and absence, but you know how good it feels each morning to see a loving face and hear a familiar voice, and know that you begin today's adventures surround by loving arms. I'm nearly sixty years older than you, Jack, and I still need the same things. Each morning when I wake up – just a few minutes before you do, and that's pretty early – I rejoice at the morning sun, the projects I need to do today, and the familiar face – Grandma Kate's - sleeping next to me. For over thirty years, Grandma has been the first face I see every morning. She is my anchor in a changing world. Because I can count on her love, I feel comfortable going on adventures that take me all over the country.

Peek-a-boo! I'm back and so are you. So let's have a great day, with enough order and enough surprise for something new and great to happen today.

Love, Grandpa Bruce

WEEK THIRTY-EIGHT

MOVING FORWARD

I just got the phone call from your dad reporting that "the little man is crawling forward!" Now that's a really big deal, and I'm excited. For awhile you've been crawling in circles or pushing yourself backward, but now you're moving ahead, really ahead.

Grandma Kate says that you're now crawling toward her and your mom and dad. You're going toward what you want in life now. Life is about forward movement. Even when you think you're going backward, you're still going forward. A Greek philosopher Heraclitus once said, "You can't step into the same waters twice." He had a wise guy student who responded, "Teacher, you can't even go into the same waters once." Life is about change. Nothing stays the same, and now you're living the dream of moving ahead in life.

Today I received some very disappointing news. I had hoped to get a job that would bring me closer to you and your parents. I was excited about the job because my office would be just a few blocks away from your home. But, I didn't get it, and now I'm feeling a little sad. I wanted to be near you and able to stop by to see you on my way to work and back home in the evening. The job involved going back to a familiar place; a place where I worked for nearly twenty years.

As much as I wanted to get the job, it might have been crawling backward for me. You can't go back to way things were or to familiar places and think they haven't changed. So when I visualize you crawling forward, I know that I need to crawl forward to my next destination, too, looking back only to get my bearings for the next adventure.

Jack, crawling forward is the next stage of your great adventure. Someday soon, you'll be walking and running. You'll still crawl from time to time. After all, I've been crawling a lot lately – just to be next to you while you learn to crawl. You don't crawl backward much now, but you can remember what it was like to crawl backward, and this will remind you to be patient with anyone who moves more slowly than you do.

So, Jack, move ahead with your life, and care for those who move more slowly, perhaps they have a longer distance to go.

Love, Grandpa Bruce

WEEK THIRTY-NINE

SEPARATION ANXIETY

The other day when I picked you up, you looked around in search of your mom and started crying. Suddenly you realized that she wasn't there and you were being held by a man you hadn't seen for a few days. Right now, you're trying figure out the sources of your nurture and protection. You're also growing in memory and experience. This time it only took you a moment to realize I was also someone familiar, the bearded man who plays with you in the morning and takes you on walks in the neighborhood.

Life is about connection and separation. At the very beginning, you are completely connected. Your home is in your mother's womb. There you receive everything you need – food, warmth, and shelter. But then, you are thrust into a bright, buzzing, and confusing world. Your mother, first, and then other significant people become the sources of nurture and protection. Your circle of life expands to embrace all sorts of new people, many of whom will love and support you.

It's alright to be reserved and to be careful about your relationships. Not everyone is trustworthy. Nor will everyone give you what you need to be healthy and happy. The story is told of the great scientist, Albert Einstein. When he was asked what the most important question in life is, Einstein answered, "Is the universe friendly?" Another great thinker, Erik Erikson, said the most important thing a baby learns is to trust the universe. You learn trust from your mother and those who provide you with nurture and care. Later, the circles of trust expand to include your dad, grandparents, and special people like your Aunt Karen. If they love you well enough, you can live with the imperfections of others, but still feel good about yourself and the world.

As you grow older, you'll learn that you are a separate, unique person who takes responsibility for his life. Hopefully, you'll also learn that you're never alone. There will always be people who will love you and respond to your deepest needs. Some people, like me, believe that God is always with us – in the cells of our bodies, in the air we breathe, in good ideas, and people we love. This gives us a sense of peace when life is confusing and changing too quickly.

In the years ahead, you'll meet new people and go on great adventures. You'll learn that some strangers can be trusted and that you'll need to keep an eye on others. But if we love you enough and teach you to be strong, you'll face the ups and downs of life with courage and creativity. You will learn to be happy when you're alone and also happy with people. You'll learn that you're never alone even when you're by yourself.

Love, Grandpa Bruce

WEEK FORTY

LOOKING BACKWARD

Being with you these days, Jack, reminds me of when your dad was a baby. He would set off crawling at a breakneck speed and then stop and look back to see where I was. Sometimes your dad and I would go to Turtle Park, a playground near American University in Washington D.C and he'd get so engrossed in playing with trucks in the sand that he'd forget I was even there. Of course, I was always watching him! Then, all of a sudden, he'd stop and look around just to make sure that I was still there.

This morning you did the same thing. You raced across the living room floor and vanished for a moment into the dining room. I followed you from a distance, crawling on all fours myself. As you reached the far corner of the dining room, you stopped, sat down, and looked backward. When you noticed me, you gave a little smile of recognition as if to say, "I'm a big boy, who can crawl really fast. But, I want to know that you're with me."

When your dad was in second grade, we decided that once in awhile it would be a good idea for him to walk to school. So for several days, he and I crossed the busy street together and then I told him to set out ahead of me. Of course, I was close by and ready to run as fast as I could just in case a car came by. At first, your dad protested. He wanted me to walk beside him. Eventually, he walked twenty feet ahead of me constantly looking back to make sure I was walking behind him. Then he walked fifty feet ahead, and finally nearly a whole block. But always, he looked back just to make sure I was there in case he needed help.

Today, your dad walks to work on his own. He goes to foreign countries like Dubai and Abu Dhabi for his job. But still he calls me to ask about important things and to tell me all the new things you are doing. I call him too when I need help. You see, Jack, we always need to know that someone is watching out for us. We need to know that if we get in trouble, somebody will drop everything and run to our side – to dry our tears, protect us from dogs, or walk beside us in a tough time.

I think that's what love's about. When you're older, you'll notice that your dad occasionally keeps an eye on me. I'm still a pretty young guy (only fifty nine), but your dad wants to make sure I'm healthy, eating the right things, and feeling alright when hard times come. I do the same for him. When he was sick a few years back, your grandma and I raced to his side, and stayed there at the hospital to remind him that we loved him and that he wasn't alone.

So, Jack, I think it's a good thing to look back. Your mom and dad will always be there for you. Their love will be a circle to protect you and help you discover new places and things. No matter how far you travel, you'll always have a home where people are watching out for you and want you to be happy.

Maybe that's what God is all about, too. Someone to watch out for us, to walk beside us even we're unaware of it, and to give us courage when we travel to new places.

So, keep looking around, my love – and God's - will go with you every step of the way.

Love, Grandpa Bruce

WEEK FORTY-ONE

ADVENTURES AT TURTLE PARK

Grandma Kate called me this morning with exciting news. The two of you played at Turtle Park all morning. Now, Turtle Park is a very special place, Jack, as I mentioned earlier. Turtle Park has one of the biggest sand boxes you'll ever play in. And it has a statue of a big turtle right in the middle of the sand box! Now that's something special.

But more than that, I used to take your dad to Turtle Park when he was a small boy. We moved to Washington DC when your dad was two and soon discovered Turtle Park. It was a safe and fun place to play for toddlers and babies. Your dad used to play there with some of the little boys and girls, who nearly thirty years later, are still your dad's best friends – Peter and Aaron and Anna. Peter's dad Bede and I used to pack the kids in the car and spend the morning at the park. Sometimes, Peter's mom, Carol, and I took your dad and Peter to the park. We'd talk and the boys would play. Once in awhile, we'd intervene when they needed a little parental direction.

Today, while I was eating lunch in Lancaster, Grandma Kate said you ran into the mother of one your dad's childhood friends, and her granddaughter, a little girl named Alana. She's about a year older than you, and her dad Avram (Avi) and your dad went to school together. You don't know this yet, but I am a minister as well as a writer and teacher. I performed the wedding for Alana's parents (Avram and Linnea) and baptized her when she was a baby.

Hearing that you were at Turtle Park brought back old memories and gave me a sense of gratitude that you are reliving some of the adventures your dad had when he was small. It's always good to do new things, but it's a joy to share some of the places that were important to your parents and grandparents.

I was even more excited when I heard another piece of news. You went down the slide! Wow! Grandma Kate held your hand, while you slid down a few feet in the small slide. And then you wanted to do it again! That's a really big adventure, Jack, and life is filled with new adventures. Even small things, like sliding a few feet, can be great adventures because they open the doors to a whole new world.

I remember that when your dad was two years old, he went down the same slide and spent hours playing with the toys at the park just like you did today. Now your dad is a big person with a little boy all his own.

All big adventures begin with a small step, or little slide! Taking that first step is the big deal. Once you've taken that step, it's easier to take the next and then the next. In a couple days, I'm coming to town and you can be sure that Grandpa and you are going to Turtle Park! And we'll go down the slide and climb on the turtle just like I did with your dad a long time ago.

Love, Grandpa Bruce

WEEK FORTY-TWO

PEOPLE AS FURNITURE

Many years ago, one of my Georgetown students coined the phrase "people as furniture" to describe people leaning against each other and sleeping on top of one another (in proper fashion) during our college student retreats. I have discovered that you not only see people as furniture but also as fun obstacles to crawl over when you're in pursuit of a rolling ball or just want to go from one place to the other.

Now, I like to lounge around and sometimes when we're playing on the floor, I lie down to rest a moment, but also to be near you if you want to bring me into your games. It seems the very moment that I lie down off you go, right at me, crawling over me on your way to your next destination. Sometimes you struggle and push your legs one way and then another until you get enough traction to boost yourself on my stomach – no small feat, let me tell you – and climb right over me as if I'm a pillow or some other object in your way. When you get stuck, I roll part way over and dump you on the other side, which always causes you to smile. Even more fun is when you crawl on top of me and we start to wrestle, making all sorts of grunting he-man noises!

I wonder what sort of adventures you imagine as you climb on top of people. Do you think of us as mountains or castle walls or trees to climb? Or just something blocking the path you've chosen?

I enjoy your climbing exploits, Jack, but what's most fun is when you sit on my lap while we read in the morning, curl up to rest a moment before your next adventure, or lean against my chest as you're falling asleep. But these moments of peace don't last forever; before you know it, you're off again in search of your next discovery. I like it when you climb over me or just sit awhile, because for a moment we're connected physically. I can give you a pat on the back, hug you a little bit, or send a little energy your way.

We're intended to have joy in welcome and safe touching, that shows us that we're loved, comforts us when we're frightened, and reminds us that arms are meant for hugging. I'm glad to be furniture for you, Jack, and to wrestle and play, and be a very big obstacle in your way. It's one of the many ways I can love you.

Love, Grandpa Bruce

WEEK FORTY-THREE

FATHER'S DAY

Today is your dad's first Father's Day. Of course, for him every day is father's day. Your dad – my son – loves you with all his heart and tries to be with you as much as possible just I tried to be present with him when he was a young boy. You're a father all your life and I still give your dad some tips and try to respond to questions he has about life and how to live well. But of course, knowing your dad, you can be sure that he tells me plenty too, about how I should watch my weight and share my thoughts with the wider world by writing a best-seller. I want to share a little bit about my dad. So let me tell some stories about my father.

I learned a lot about being a father from my dad, Everett Lewis Epperly (1910-2003) and hopefully have passed some of his loving care along to you and your dad. My dad was a small town pastor. He led a church – preaching sermons on Sundays, visiting the sick, and helping people in need. He was never a great success in the eyes of the world, but he was the most important person in my life as a child. Probably my dad, along with your Grandma Kate, is the person who shaped me most as person. I am sure that I found my life's work as a theologian and pastor as a result of the values of reflection, study, and love of God that I received from my dad when I was a boy and later as a college student and adult.

Three activities typify my appreciation for my dad. Books, Baseball, and Walking! My dad and I were early risers and every morning before my brother and mom awakened, we would read together – baseball books, Hardy Boys' mysteries, adventure books. The one book I remember most was the reading John Steinbeck's *Travels with Charlie* in 1961. The plot involved Steinbeck driving around America with a camper mounted on his truck, accompanied by his poodle, Charlie. Before it became a book, it was serialized in *Holiday* magazine. My dad picked up the magazine at the local library at the end of each month, the first day you could check them out – and I could hardly wait for him to come home with the latest edition! Then, we'd slowly read through the text until the next edition came out. Fifty years have passed and I still treasure those early mornings with my dad. I suspect I became a reader and writer, in part, because of my dad's love of words – written, spoken, and preached.

When I became a father, your dad and I read each morning – mysteries, action adventures, and the sports page. We also read every night just before bed. We even read *Travels with Charlie* when your dad was ten years old! These days, he reads with you – his own nine month old son – but not first thing in the morning. Like me, you're an early riser, so when I'm at your house we always read *Dinosaur Friends in Living Color*. We talk about the "green dinosaurs' teeth" or the "purple dinosaur" with splashes – yes splashes! – of yellow on the side of his body. Later in the morning, we sit together watching the PBS kid's show, *Dinosaur Train*, the only TV show your parents let you watch.

This morning, Father's Day, your father called me up at 6:45 a.m. and reported that the two of you were reading about a dinosaur with squiggles on his side!

My dad and I played baseball – catch, balls and strikes, and three flies up. One Christmas, my dad built a backstop made of chicken wire and planks of wood at the church, and then on Christmas Eve, walked the backstop the two blocks from our church to our home. History repeated itself with your dad.

109

When he was a young guy, we spent hours playing catch or hitting the ball around in the back yard. Just like my childhood home, our big backyard became the neighborhood ball field.

My dad and I walked. I've always loved walking, and when I was in college, my dad and I began to take evening walks in our neighborhood and Saturday walks on the rugged trails of Alum Rock Park in the San Jose, California, foothills. It just seemed natural that when your dad grew up, he and I would become walkers. Sometimes we take you on walks with you in your stroller. But, often it's just two of us – me and your dad, father and son, walking two miles to my son's – your dad's - office in Washington DC or meeting one another on his walk home from work. My dad and I often talked theology; your dad and I talk politics and foreign affairs.

What I'm trying to tell you, Jack, is what a joy it is to be a parent or a grandparent, and how the best times of life happen without any fanfare or drama. Sure, you'll love going with your dad to Disney World and to the see the Washington Nationals play baseball or the Georgetown Hoyas play basketball, but the best moments often happen when you're doing everyday things – reading good night stories, driving to the market, watching a game together, or just playing catch or kicking the soccer ball. Of course, there will be lots of special everyday moments of love with your mom, too!

I am grateful for my dad and for having the opportunity to be an everyday dad to my son, your dad. I know you already know your dad's love and I hope it grows in all sorts of ways in the future. Someday, you may remember what it was like to be with your dad as you play with your own little boy or girl. The circle of love grows larger and spirals forth from generation to generation.

Love, Grandpa Bruce

WEEK FORTY-FOUR

LICKING GRANDPA'S NOSE

You come from a very affectionate family. Your parents and grandparents, along with your caregiver Maria, give you lots of hugs and kisses. You receive the fullness of love all day long. But this week, you started kissing back. Well, sort of. You came close to my face, stuck out your tongue, and then licked my nose - a big wet lick, almost like a puppy dog. And then, you smiled. You knew what you'd done and were rewarded by a kiss from Grandpa. Later that day, I heard you also licked your mom and dad's noses as well as Grandma's nose. You were sharing what you received – all the love your little heart could hold.

I could tell, at that moment, that you are going to follow in the footsteps of your dad. As you grow older, you'll become a man of affection and passion, someone who will give as well as receive love. Sharing the love in your heart is one of the most important things in life. Right now, your baby heart is a big one. It's been nurtured by love and that great love is flowing through you to the whole world. Your baby heart is filled with love, joy, and affection, and now you're learning to share the love you've received.

My prayer is that your heart will always be filled with love and sharing this love will always be easy for you. As you grow older, you'll learn that a lot of people have trouble sharing their love, and even more people feel unloved and have no one with whom to share their deepest affections. But I know you will love and show that love in ways that are good and healthy and affirmative of others.

In the meantime, your mom, dad, grandma and me, will protect and nourish your baby heart, and give you all the love we have. We'll love each other, too, so you'll know what it means to care for one another through all the joys and sorrows of life. From the love you are receiving, you'll learn to be a man who loves deeply, who is loyal to your friends, and faithful to your life partner.

Love, Grandpa Bruce

WEEK FORTY-FIVE

THE BIG NOISE

Yesterday, Maria told me you heard a loud noise. The carbon monoxide alarm went off with all the bells, whistles, and warnings. Your nanny, Maria ,told me that you were really frightened and had trouble getting to sleep later that night. I know the feeling, Jack - sometimes you hear something and the rest of the day you're feeling upset and off kilter.

Now, there are a lot of scary things in the world. Even adults feel anxious at times. Some threats you imagine and some threats are real, but they still can keep you up at night. A few weeks ago I couldn't sleep. I was nervous about a job interview I was having the next day, and started to feel anxious and short of breath. And I got anxious because I was feeling anxious. That may not make sense, but sometimes knowing we feel bad can make us feel worse, because we think we can't do anything about it. But your Grandma Kate stayed up until I felt better. Your grandma and I take care of each other when we're feeling scared and need someone to hold our hand.

When your dad was small, he had trouble getting to sleep. When he went to sleep, he had bad dreams. He felt so scared that he just couldn't sleep. Sometimes he had to crawl in bed with us until he fell asleep. Your grandma and I were worried and so we took him to see Dr. K. He had your dad draw some pictures and then they talked awhile. Dr. K. gave your dad and us some advice that I've followed now for nearly twenty five years – "It's alright to be afraid, but you don't need to be afraid of being afraid."

You'll discover in the years to come that you'll be frightened by a lot of things. Sometimes it will be your imagination. Other times you'll be scared for a good reason. Life is good, and most people are caring and decent. Most of the bad things that you imagine happening, you or your loved ones can respond to, but every so often, things are scary and you need to be cautious. You need to find someone to help you out. You may need to find someone to protect you or be your advocate. You may have to protect or advocate for others who can't speak for themselves or who have been hurt by others.

But remember, Jack, the night that the alarm went off, Maria held you in her arms till you fell asleep. Then, your mom and dad came home and were with you when you woke up the next morning, safe and sound. There will always be people you can count on when you feel frightened – Mom and Dad, Grandma and Grandpa, and Maria. When you're older, you'll have special friends who will be there for you in good times and bad. When the night is dark and you hear strange noises, they'll hold your hand and give you hugs, and you'll know that everything's going to be alright.

Love, Grandpa Bruce

WEEK FORTY-SIX

SMILING WHEN YOU WAKE UP

I've said this several times throughout the book, because it typifies our relationship: both of us love the morning. We like to get up before everyone else and play together. Right now, you like to wake up about 5:00 a.m. every morning. I make it a point, when I'm staying at your home, to get up before you and instead of taking my morning walk, I listen for you to wake up and greet you with a smile, change your diaper, and get you ready for the day. Your mom and dad have a baby monitor in the living room, so I can hear you rustling around your bed, then talking to yourself, and finally announcing with a cry, "I'm up. Where's everyone else. I want company!"

When I opened the door of your room this morning, there you were, standing up and leaning against the rail of your crib, with a smile as wide as your face. It's such a wonderful sight – to see you smiling as you greet a new day along with your grandpa.

I'm glad you wake up happy and ready for today's adventures. It's good to begin the day with joy, because each morning is new and filled with possibilities. I'm like you, Jack. I wake up each morning with the same verse from the Bible, "This is the day that God has made and I will rejoice and be glad in it!" (Psalm 118:24) and then ask myself a question, "What interesting or challenging thing will happen today? What great thing will I do today?" While some of my days seem pretty routine and appear to have no great surprises, I find that each day brings something new into my life and many opportunities to learn new things and grow as a person.

We're both growing as people, Jack. For you, it's all adventure as you speed crawl across the living room, discover how interesting a computer keyboard can be, follow the flight of a bird, or express your feelings in a new way. That's the way it should be: greeting each day as an adventure.

Each day really is an adventure. Sometimes grownups get into a rut, and I think it's sad that many people quit wanting to learn new things as they grow older. They don't read or go to new places or meet new people. They forget that life is about growth and leaving the familiar. But, that's not us, Jack. We are people who are curious, who want to be surprised by new ideas and new possibilities.

When your dad was about two years old, Great Grandma Max, his grandmother, bought a picture frame that said above his picture, "Look out world, here I come." That's a good way to look at life. To see the world as an exciting place, and embrace something new every day.

Your life is going to be exciting, Jack. When I look at nearly six decades of living, I'm amazed at all that's happened. When I was a little boy, I never imagined what life would bring. I never imagined I'd be a writer or travel to other countries. We used typewriters and not computers when I was in college. I never owned a cell phone until I was in my late forties. We didn't know anything about ecology or global climate change when I was a child. No one thought China or Japan would become great economic powers. Believe it or not, in those days, long before Grandma and I bought our Toyota Highlander, "made in Japan" meant cheap and junky! I remember the excitement of watching the first human walking on the moon. All these things are normal for you, Jack.

You'll have great adventures, Jack. Life will always be interesting if you greet the world with a smile and arms open to the world in all its wonder and surprise.

Love, Grandpa Bruce

WEEK FORTY-SEVEN

POINTING

The last few weeks you've been pointing at everything – the ceiling fan, birds, bushes, trees, cars, and people. Pointing is a good thing. It means you're interested in the world and want to find out what things are and how they work. When your dad was about eighteen months old, he began to point at everything as he asked "Dat? Dat? Dat?" At first, I didn't know what he meant, but then I realized he was saying, "What's that? What's that? What's that?" Sometimes your dad would repeat "Dat" twenty times in a row as he pointed at things on the street or in our home.

It is a great gift to want to know things. This is a wonderful time for you to be alive, Jack. You're learning amazing things every day. You're beginning to learn adult language and speak our words in your own way. You're pretty smart and have a big vocabulary already. We're the ones who can't figure it out!

Yes, pointing is a good thing. It means you're not afraid to ask questions. Sometimes adults are afraid to ask questions. They think they'll sound silly or stupid. So they act like they know things, when they haven't a clue, just because they won't ask.

Nowadays, I'm feeling younger spiritually and relationally, although my beard is getting whiter and my hair thinner. You're teaching me that asking questions – or pointing out things I don't know – is an important way to learn new things.

There's so much you don't know, Jack, and pointing is one way to learn. There's so much I don't know and asking questions helps me learn, too.

I'm learning something about pointing, too. I'm discovering that I need to be at your level to really know the things that are important to you. So, I sit beside you as you stand or put my head next to yours. Then I can see things from your perspective, that way we're both seeing the same things. I can mirror your world because I share it. I'm learning again what it's like to be small and have flowers and chairs at eye level. I'm also learning how faraway a lamp can be when you're small. I'm recognizing the colors of the cars that catch your eye.

It's funny that adults tend to learn fewer things as they grow older. They become content with things as they are. As I've said throughout the book, one of the greatest gifts in life is curiosity and the desire to keep growing and learning new things every day. Today, Jack, you learned hundreds of things just by living. I'm learning right beside you. My prayer is that you never quit pointing and, in the spirit of your dad, you always ask "Dat? Dat? Dat?"

Love, Grandpa Bruce

WEEK FORTY-EIGHT

THE AMAZING RACE

It happens so quickly. A week ago you were cruising around the chairs and tables, holding on with one hand while maneuvering with the other. Three days ago, you took your first steps, and now you're walking from one side of the room to the other, gaining confidence with each new step. You even stood up and pushed a ball around the room with one of the golf clubs your Grandpa Bill gave you. All of these changes happened in just one week. You may be a real handful when we take the plane trip to California next week.

Now that you're walking, Jack, I have to move quickly just to make sure that you're not getting into any trouble. I can't just be a couch potato observing your behavior. I need to be ready to spring into action at any moment. Your parents have child-proofed the house and put up baby gates at strategic places, but an inventive toddler can discover things his or her parents and grandparents can't even imagine. Now, no computer or cell phone is safe around the house. You want to type and use the phone and change the channels on TV and seem ready – and able – to grab onto any device that's in arm's reach. Much to our chagrin, you pushed a few buttons, dialing 9-1-1. We caught it just in time! The other day your Grandma Kate forgot to latch the baby gate and off you went up the stairs. (Of course, your ever-vigilant grandma caught you as you mounted the first stair.)

Walking is – no pun intended – a big step in growing up! You're beginning a path that will lead to running and jumping and hiking, maybe even skiing, golfing, and playing tennis, soccer, and baseball. You'll be able to run down the basketball court and, later on, take a walk with your first love, all because of what happened this week.

Life is, as I've said earlier, about expanding your circles of adventure. It's about starting where you are, sleeping in your mother's arms, and imagining the possibilities of going to places whose names you won't be able to pronounce for years.

I am a walker, Jack. I try to walk several miles each day, weather permitting. For me, walking is a spiritual act. An ancient saying goes "it will be solved in the walking." When I walk, new and creative ideas come to me, just like they're coming to you right now, Jack. My dad and I walked when I was in college, and I regularly take walks with your dad. I'm looking forward to walking with you, Jack. I can imagine us talking about sports and the world while we walk around the neighborhood. We will walk to baseball games and on the golf course. We will walk in the woods and mountains, filling our eyes with beauty all because of your taking these first tentative steps today!

Your circle of adventure is expanding with each new day, Jack. Your adventures will continue, growing literally and fig-uratively, in leaps and bounds, and I can only imagine all the wonderful places you'll go.

Love, Grandpa Bruce

WEEK FORTY-NINE

UP IN THE AIR

Today, we flew coast to coast, from Washington DC to Los Angeles. It was an amazing day. Six hours in the air at 30,000 feet. We're heading for the wedding of one of Matt's childhood friends and then an adventure, driving up the California coast. What a day it was! You met all sorts of people, played games with your mom and dad and your grandma and me. Like everything else you do these days, Jack, you threw yourself into the experience of flying, enjoying each moment without any sense of fear.

A lot of adults are afraid of flying. They close their eyes, clutch the arms of their seats, and hope for the best at take-off and landing. Flying is an act of trust. Up in the air with no support and nothing to hang onto! It can be scary, especially when you fly through a storm and the plane is tossed up and down like one of your toys. But these days, Jack, you fearlessly reach out to the world, just like you did when you let the waves splash over you at the beach. Of course, your dad and grandpa were holding you tight. But after that first wave, you toddled toward the ocean, filled with joy and ready to plunge into the surf again and again.

This was your second plane trip and I suspect that you'll be a global traveler in the years ahead, going places with your parents and us, and later on your own. Maybe you'll even travel to another planet. You're an adventurer, Jack, and may you always embrace new things with enthusiasm and courage.

Being in a storm can be frightening when there's only air beneath your wings, but when you trust the air and the pilot to keep you up, you'll be able to face any challenge, not just when you're flying but in every aspect of life. I believe that we are always in the circle of God's care and protection, and like the air beneath us, we will be safe regardless of what happens.

There's a children's book by Dr. Suess, entitled *Oh! The Places You'll Go*. I think Dr. Suess is right. When I was a boy, I never imagined that I'd hike in Scotland, appear on national television, write books, and speak in front of thousands of people. Each time, I needed to believe that I had the courage, creativity, and talent to succeed. I had to believe that there were forces that were on my side to give me everything I needed.

So trust the elements to hold you up, Jack. You'll have what you'll need to weather the storms, and we'll be right beside you all the way.

Love, Grandpa Bruce

WEEK FIFTY

CALIFORNIA DREAMIN'

They say anything's possible in California, and I believe that it's true. I was born in California nearly sixty years ago. I remember my adventures as a little boy growing up in the Salinas Valley, playing cowboys and Indians, Little League baseball, and imagining I could be an astronaut, firefighter, Major League ball player, and trail boss of a wagon train. My heroes were a young Clint Eastwood ("Rowdy Yates," the ramrod on the TV show *Rawhide*), Willie Mays, the centerfielder on the San Francisco Giants, Sandy Koufax who pitched for the Los Angeles Dodgers, Dick Groat who played short stop for the 1960 World Champion Pittsburgh Pirates and won the batting title that same year, and Arnold Palmer, whose risk taking approach to golf brought the game to the center stage long before Tiger Woods was born.

As a teenager and college student, I dreamed of a new world – of peace, love, and harmony. With enough love, I believed that we might usher in the Age of Aquarius. I'm still waiting for this. Though I've lived on the East Coast for nearly thirty years, I'm still a Californian in spirit – playful, imaginative, and not one to follow the "rules" unless I have to. I still push the edges – but nowadays it's in dreams of ways people can be happier and healthier and closer to the Spirit of Life. Still, I embrace novelty and possibility, and dream of that Age of Peace and Harmony.

Babies are born with the California spirit. They embrace wonder and possibility and plunge forward with no thought of safety just like you did this morning, our last day in California. You crawled off the bed and fell head first – luckily – into Grandpa's arms.

California has been a time of adventure for all of us. It was your first great trip as a child who could intentionally interact with the world. When you went to Florida at three months of age, you still were pretty much in mom and dad's arms. But now you can walk, crawl, flirt, and communicate. You make friends wherever you go, especially with women. I've noticed that you raise your eyebrows almost like a wink when one takes interest in you!

In our nine day adventure from Los Angeles to San Francisco, you discovered a new world. First, you discovered the meaning of flexibility. You entered a new time zone in which your normal bedtime was the middle of the afternoon. Though it wasn't always easy, you stayed up late some days (almost 8:00 p.m. Pacific, which is 11:00 p.m. Eastern). You still got up early, and that was our time, of course.

Flexibility is essential to a good life. Being able to adapt to new situations, to have a vision of the future but know what's needed right now, and to take into consideration other people's feelings and visions.

A lot of adults have trouble being flexible. They think compromise and change are bad things. This past week our nation's leaders had trouble making some important decisions because some of our leaders wouldn't give up their positions for the welfare of the nation. They almost took our country off a cliff – like a baby falling off a bed – because they couldn't or wouldn't see the big picture. They had small ideas, when only big dreams can rebuild our nation! As you grow older, Jack, you'll realize that your dreams need to touch the ground and that means you have to be flexible. Know what you want, hold onto your dreams, but also listen to others. This isn't "getting along by going along." It's moving ahead by building teams.

Flexibility is about willingness to change and that's what you've done this week. You changed from a crawler to a toddler who could take ten steps, to a child that could take a hundred paces without falling. Wow! Now I have to work hard to keep up with you, Jack. At our hotel in Carmel, you walked the length of the croquet court several times, wearing your grandpa out as we rolled the croquet ball across the lawn.

This week we both learned that you are quite a gourmet. You discovered you have a wide palette. You enjoyed omelets with cheese and pesto, brioche, pancakes, French toast, pineapple, Eggs Benedict, and clam chowder.

This week you also met the ocean and you both lived to tell the story. You couldn't get enough of the waves, fearlessly meeting them as they crashed against your knees. Of course we held your hands. But still you were very brave. It's always best, you see, to try new things with people you can trust, and who will make sure you're safe and help you succeed when you try something new. As you'll discover later in life, courage and creativity are inner virtues that are also nurtured by going into the unknown and trying new things one step at a time.

There's so much more that I could say about our California adventure, Jack. More important, than anything on this trip you'll only remember through the films and photos we took, is the adventure itself. You can always imagine new things and make them happen. You can constantly push the limits of discovery and creativity. Don't let the world squeeze you into a pre-cut mold, but color outside the lines, embracing new ideas, new people, and new ways of life. That's the California spirit! That's the spirit of adventure that makes every day exciting and each encounter an opportunity for learning new things.

Love, Grandpa Bruce

FIFTY-ONE

THE "NO" THAT SAYS "YES"

You are beginning to hear the word "no" and that isn't always fun for parents and grandparents and toddlers. Life is filled with infinite possibilities but they aren't always good for you or others. I know that you don't like hearing the word "no," Jack, and I don't like saying it, but hearing the word "no" is part of growing up. At your age, it involves learning what is safe and what is unsafe, and what is good for you and what isn't. You weren't happy when I told you not to touch the fireplace at the Lodge in Half Moon Bay. You even cried a little bit. But, some "no's" are good for you. You can burn your hands when you touch a fireplace or stove.

Whenever we travel, we try to put safety plugs on electrical outlets, and this week you tried to pull them all off. I had to tell you "no" and you gave me a pouty face. But, the biggest "no's" have come in the last few weeks now that you've been teething. You have ten teeth and counting and sometimes you just want the comfort of gnawing on something. That's ok if it's a chew toy or a cloth, but not if it's Mommy's hand or Grandma's shoulder. Then, it just plain hurts. Ouch! And then, we tell you. Sometimes you cry, because you want to be a really good boy and you're used to so many "yeses" in life. Other times, I think you just want to chew and are unhappy when we place a limit on you.

You might recall that I said earlier in this book that the word "no" is an important part of life. Limits are good even in a world of possibilities because they help us respect other peoples' bodies and property. Limits are also about being polite. I know some adults who believe that they can say everything they think. They call themselves "frank" or "truthful" when they really are impolite and hurtful. I have learned that words are meant to help, connect, and support. They are meant to express important thoughts and feelings.

Sometimes we have to say "no" to other people – to tell them they've hurt us or made a mistake that could hurt them, but still we tell the truth with the goal of caring for the other person.

A good life involves the right balance of "yes" and "no." In my work, marriage, and relationships, I try to say a lot of "yeses." I try to encourage people to be creative and bold – to risk making mistakes for a greater good. I try to tell people they're doing good work. Still, I need to say "no" or point it out when people have gone too far or crossed a line that hurt me or another person or a project we're working on. But my goal is always to say a lot more "yeses" than "no's."

I know that you will push the limits, Jack, and that's part of being an adventurer. Sometimes, I will push back and tell you "no" or "you can't do that now" or "that will hurt you." I want you to listen to me, because when I say "no," it's not about me, it's about what's best for you. You need to trust my judgment and love.

As you get older, we will quit saying "no" about some things, and begin to say "no" about others. We won't worry about you sticking your hand in a light socket, but we will worry about you crossing the street without looking or going places without telling us. Later, we'll place limits about how late you can stay out at night or when you can drive the car. We'll tell you not to drink alcohol or take drugs, or get into a car with people who have been drinking or taking drugs. This is all to keep you safe and healthy and strong. It's the "no" that says "yes." You won't like it at first, but this is all part of the growing process. It helps you stay healthy and live creatively with your loved ones.

Love, Grandpa Bruce

WEEK FIFTY-TWO

MODELING

Jack, you're getting to be a big boy. Every day is an adventure. Every day is an opportunity to explore your known universe and then go places you've never been before.

One of the things I've noticed lately is that you're always watching and listening. You watch your mom and dad, other children, especially bigger kids, and you watch Grandma and me. You're beginning to imitate the words we say, making sounds that communicate what you want. You're learning games from us and patterns of behavior from us — and sometimes quite quickly!

A few weeks ago, Grandma Kate beat on her chest. Within an hour, you beat a rhythm on my chest and you enjoyed it! I gave you a kiss on the cheek and you tried to kiss me back. Your dad puts a square shape in a square hole and then you do it. I hit a ball with another ball and you immediately do the same thing.

We learn a lot from each other. Imitation is a good thing. We learn new things first by observing and then by doing. Sometimes we're a little clumsy at first, but after awhile we get the hang of it.

Now we adults model certain things and even though you don't have words yet for what we do, you sure do notice. That means we have to be careful as well as creative. I have to remember the "right" words for "poop." I have to watch what I say when I stub my toe. Of course we'll slip sometimes and you'll add to your vocabulary words we never intended for you to learn – though we know you'll learn them eventually in school and with friends.

Still we adults need to remind ourselves how important we are as models for your learning and living. We need to show you what love means. We need to demonstrate how to solve problems and respond to stress in ways that are helpful and healthy. We need to let you know that it's ok not to get your own way all the time. We need to model patience and forgiveness and sacrifice when things aren't going well. We need to deal with conflict in ways that help everyone get what they really need and respect other people's feelings. We need to aspire to being better persons so that you can be a person of generosity, love, and courage.

These days, Jack, you're all ears and all eyes and that's good. The world has so much to teach you and we want to teach you as well, so that when you're older you'll grow into a young man who knows how to love and share and look out for other people as well as yourself. If we are at our best now, then you'll always be at your best, too.

Love, Grandpa Bruce

AN AMAZING ADVENTURE

THE FIRST BIRTHDAY

So glad you're here, so glad you're here
So glad you're here, today.
Love brought us here, love brought us here,
Love brought us here, today.

Well, Jack, you'll probably never remember you're first year. But oh, what an adventure it's been. The adventure continues. We have grown together, an aging baby boomer and his little grandchild, learning so many new things along the way. I have rediscovered the parenting skills – now, as a grandparent – I learned first of all when your dad was a baby. I have gained a personal relationship with diapers, onesies, organic formula, and our favorite book, *Dinosaur Friends in Living Color*. I regularly invoke Dr. Scott the paleontologist and sing *Dinosaur Train* with you.

I have followed your adventure from living entirely on mother's milk to discovering that you like pesto and omelets and pineapple. You've become quite a gourmet. You are tasting and seeing how good this life can be.

I have crawled on all fours alongside you and now I have to run to keep up with you. I am amazed at how quickly you grow, as if impelled by an inner wisdom or perhaps that angel whispering in your cells, "grow, grow." One day you walk three steps; a week later you take one hundred paces across the croquet court at the resort in Carmel. One day you refuse the bottle, and only a few months later, you smack your lips as you sample brioche, blueberries, salmon, and guacamole.

The creative wisdom that energizes your cells is also enlightening your soul. First, you learned about love by being fed and held. Now, you are returning love as you cuddle and kiss, though once in awhile like a teenage Romeo, you leave a bite mark! You are slowly learning that the world is populated with other people who place limits on you, but also love and protect you. You are discovering the uniqueness of all your "special" people and treat each of us – Mom, Dad, Grandma, and Grandpa – in your own unique way.

This week, I had the joy of spending two days with you. Maria was sick and Grandpa needed to be a nanny! We went to the park, met friends at Wesley Theological Seminary, ate at Chicken Out, Le Pain Quotidian, and had a snack at Starbucks. You fell asleep in the car, and I lovingly watched you as I sat in the backseat beside you, reading my book.

The day before your birthday, something strange happened – there was an earthquake near Washington D.C. It wasn't a big one, but people were anxious, because earthquakes just don't happen in our nation's capitol. We didn't feel it, because we were driving in the car. Your mom and dad tried to call me, but the phone lines were overloaded.

Life can shake you up, Jack, and it will continue to shake you up in the year ahead as you go new places and try new things. It will feel like an earthquake with all the changes ahead, some good and some bad. But we will be by your side and do all we can to make sure the changes help you grow. We will do all we can to make sure you're safe when the earth shakes.

Three hundred sixty five days, each new day bringing something new and surprising. Each morning has been filled with possibilities beyond numbering. Who knows what adventures

await as you toddle on to your second year? You are my sunshine, my little man Jack, and your little soul surely shines.
  Love to you, Jack, on your birthday and every day,

Grandpa Bruce

Also by Bruce Epperly

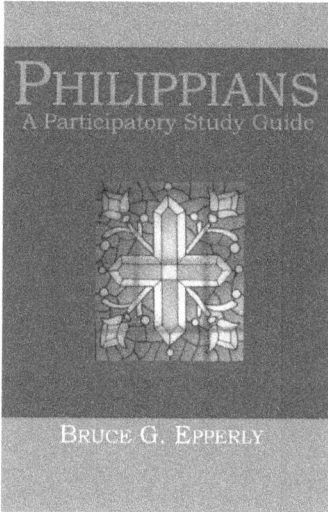

PHILIPPIANS
A Participatory Study Guide

BRUCE G. EPPERLY

Bruce Epperly is an able co-conspirator of the Spirit and the church, leading us through Philippians to find the joy of the high calling of Christ Jesus.

Rev. Dr. George A. Mason
Senior Pastor
Wilshire Baptist Church
Dallas, Texas

To read *Transforming Acts* is to go on a journey with a deeply-attuned, thoughtful and progressive thinker and theologian.

Rev. Kathy Harvey Nelson
Director of the Center for
Leadership Development
Lancaster Theological Seminary
Lancaster, PA

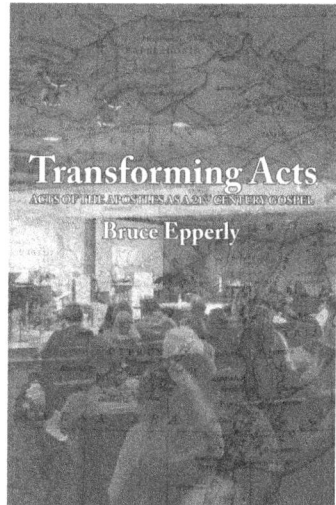

Transforming Acts
Bruce Epperly

MORE FROM ENERGION PUBLICATIONS

Personal Study
Finding My Way in Christianity	Herold Weiss	$16.99
The Sacred Journey	Chris Surber	$11.99

Christian Living
Faith in the Public Square	Robert D. Cornwall	$16.99
Grief: Finding the Candle of Light	Jody Neufeld	$8.99
Victim No More	Shauna Hyde	$12.99

Bible Study
Learning and Living Scripture	Lentz/Neufeld	$12.99
Luke: A Participatory Study Guide	Geoffrey Lentz	$8.99
Philippians: A Participatory Study Guide	Bruce Epperly	$9.99
Ephesians: A Participatory Study Guide	Robert D. Cornwall	$9.99
From Inspiration to Understanding	Edward W. H. Vick	$24.99

Theology
Creation in Scripture	Herold Weiss	$12.99
Creation: the Christian Doctrine	Edward W. H. Vick	$12.99
The Politics of Witness	Allan R. Bevere	$9.99
Ultimate Allegiance	Robert D. Cornwall	$9.99
Philosophy for Believers	Edward W. H. Vick	$14.99
The Journey to the Undiscovered Country	William Powell Tuck	$9.99
Eschatology: A Participatory Study Guide	Edward W. H. Vick	$9.99
Worshiping with Charles Darwin	Robert D. Cornwall	$9.99

Ministry
Clergy Table Talk	Kent Ira Groff	$9.99
Healing Marks	Bruce Epperly	$14.99
Wind and Whirlwind	David Moffett-Moore	$9.99
Soup Kitchen for the Soul	Renee Crosby	$12.99
Transforming Acts	Bruce Epperly	$14.99
Unfettered Spirit	Robert D. Cornwall	$14.99

Generous Quantity Discounts Available
Dealer Inquiries Welcome
Energion Publications — P.O. Box 841
Gonzalez, FL_ 32560
Website: http://energionpubs.com
Phone: (850) 525-3916